Old School is Good School

D0733565

Copyright © 2011 by Kevin G. Slater

Illustrations by David L. Slater

Old School is Good School

Cataloging-in-Publication Data

Slater, Kevin G., 1964-

Old School is Good School: 'Back to Basics'

Leadership Lessons / 1st ed.

ISBN: 978-1467912921

ASIN: B006ERVG24

PREFACE

Although my alarm clock obnoxiously screeches to life at an early hour every day, it's not what gets me out of bed. It definitely wakes me up, but it's not what gets me out of bed. What does get me out of bed every morning? My sense of purpose does. Where did I get this priceless gift? I got it from Air Force leaders. I fine tune it every day by watching and listening to my subordinates, my peers, and my leaders.

During my nearly three decades in uniform, inspirational leaders instilled in me the belief that I'm not getting out of bed just to go do a job. I'm getting out of bed to influence my world. How did they deliver this sense of purpose to me? By telling me and then showing me what makes my service far different than just a job.

First they introduced me to clear behavioral expectations and said they apply to every Airman (enlisted, officer, and civilian). They not only explained how important it was I understand these expectations, they also modeled these behaviors for me through their actions—they showed me the way.

Then they introduced me to accountability. Did they set high standards? Definitely. Did they believe high standards were important? Certainly. Did they believe there was one thing more important than high standards? Absolutely! ... Accountability! They believed high standards were worthless without enforcement ... without accountability.

They never once apologized for holding me or anyone else accountable. In fact, funny thing is, I never once expected them to.

Finally they wanted me to understand what made me different. They'd tell me all the time, "not just anyone can do what we do. Not just anyone can be an American Airman." They taught me about teamwork, shared commitment, and uncommon purpose. They taught me few people are willing to subjugate their personal goals to those of their team and even fewer are willing to lay down their life to defend and advance our ideals. They led me to embrace our core values of Integrity First, Service-Before-Self, and Excellence In All We Do. These values set the tone for everything we are as citizens and as Airmen. Every Airman has a purpose, not a job.

Each morning, when my feet hit the floor, I'm thankful my leaders took the time to instill in me a sense of purpose; a broader understanding of the bigger picture; the answer to the proverbial question, why am I here? Alarm clock? 20 bucks. Sense of purpose? Priceless!

INTRODUCTION

At every level of formal training and professional military education American Airmen learn to embrace the United States Air Force core values of Integrity First, Service-Before-Self, and Excellence In All We Do. Our values inspire and guide our Airmen to give their best effort toward every duty, without favor to personal desire, even under the most demanding of circumstances. Our core values fuel a sense of purpose which drives America's Airmen to Fly, Fight, and Win in Air, Space, and Cyberspace.

Throughout my career, I have penned NOTAMs[1] (Notice to Airmen) or anecdotes delivering leadership and followership lessons to my peers and subordinates based on events from the life of an Airman. Although my career as an American Airman is the genesis of these anecdotes, I'm convinced the leadership and followership lessons they provide are universally useful to leaders and followers from all walks of life.

---

[1] Notice to Airmen (NOTAM) - a messaging tool used in the global aviation community to alert pilots to hazards enroute to or at a specific location

CONTENTS

PREFACE   iii
INTRODUCTION   v

Chapter 1   INTEGRITY FIRST

                   Airman with a Capital 'A'   9
                   Backbone of the Air Force   11
                   You Get What You Tolerate   14
                   Remedial Training   17
                   Bones   21
                   Expectation Not Reward   23
                   Give 'em HELL   26
                   I've Got Your Back   28
                   The Least We Can Do   31
                   Cato Leads The Way   34
                   Be the Good Boss   38
                   My Two Favorite Questions   40
                   A Little More Than Duty   42

Chapter 2   SERVICE-BEFORE-SELF

                   Followership   45
                   Commitment   48
                   Travel in Uniform   50
                   Professional Courtesy   53
                   Put Me In Coach   56
                   Best When On   58
                   Bumper Cars   60
                   MSF Training Rules!   63
                   Good Pain   65
                   I'm Impressed   68
                   Right 10, Left 32, Right 18   71

Being Mr. Underwood   73
When is a Wall not a Wall?   75
Promotion Test 'No-Show'   77
Reenlistment Bonuses: Good for All   79
Legacy   81
The Birth of our Nation   83
Our Flag: Long May She Wave   86
A Proud Heritage   88
Avoid 'Coulda, Shoulda, Woulda'   90

Chapter 3   EXCELLENCE IN ALL WE DO

Belief: A High Performance Fuel   93
My Mess Dress Got Promoted Today   96
You See It, You Own It   98
You Own Your Own Morale   101
PGA Pro and PB&J   103
Never Failed? Trying Hard Enough?   106
Seize Your Opportunity   109
They're On My Feet   111
A 40-inch Waist or Waste?   113
Starship Troopers   116
The Whole Person Concept   118
Slay Promotion Myths   121
Embrace Development Expectations   124
Reading is Fundamental   127
Grasp the Baton of Enlisted History   129
Our Proud Air Force History   131
Why are Windshields Larger   133
than Rear View Mirrors?

CONCLUSION   135
ACKNOWLEDGMENTS   142

I am responsible and accountable for my duty
and my actions. My word is my bond.

Chapter 1

INTEGRITY FIRST

The moral courage to do what is right even if the
personal cost is high.

<u>Airman with a Capital 'A'</u>

In 2004, General John P. Jumper, then Air Force Chief of Staff, pronounced in a message to our force, "That's Airman with a capital A!" What was his point? One letter at the beginning of a word can mean a great deal. We learn as children a capital letter at the start of a word signifies something special or important, like our own name, our hometown, or our country. Our Airmen are the heart and soul of our unique fighting force and deserve to be recognized by a proper noun too, thus **earning** the capital 'A'.

In 2006, General T. Michael Moseley, then Air Force Chief of Staff, and our 15th Chief Master Sergeant of the Air Force Rod McKinley emphasized the next logical step—asking each of us to take pride in referring to each other as Airmen and not as 'troops' or 'kids'. I've caught myself more than a few times referring to some of our youngest Airmen as 'kids' and have worked hard to correct myself, I urge each of you to consider doing the same.

Did you know recruits are no longer referred to as Airmen when they arrive at Air Force Basic Military Training? They are 'trainees' until they earn the **privilege** to be called Airman. Each trainee is expected to learn our history and to gain an appreciation of our heritage—in other words learn what it means to join our profession of arms. Every trainee works very hard to build the physical and mental capacity to master the warfighting skills required for membership in our elite air, space, and cyberspace force. Only then does a trainee **earn** the title of Airman. This honor is granted as part of an Airman's coin ceremony conducted the day prior to every graduation parade. This ceremonial transition of trainee to Airman is such a powerful experience I rarely see a dry eye in the formation of Airmen or in the reviewing stands filled with hundreds of proud family members.

Our service and our nation ask much from those who earn the title Airman. Tens of thousands of warrior Airmen are engaged in-garrison and around the globe to fly, fight, and win; to serve as our nation's sword and shield; its sentry and avenger; to defend our country with their life; to never leave an Airman behind, to never falter, and to not fail. Let's not risk miscommunicating, or inadvertently downplaying, the value or contribution of our Airmen by referring to them as 'troops' or 'kids'.

I'm faithful to a proud heritage and legacy of valor established by those who've gone before me. I'm privileged to be an Airman with a capital 'A'. Feel free to refer to me as one anytime!

Backbone of the Air Force

I still remember the first time I heard a General Officer declare, "The Noncommissioned Officer (NCO)[1] Corps is the backbone of the Air Force." I regarded this as high praise and was curious to know why the General was such a fan of the NCO Corps. Following his closing remarks at an event many years ago, I approached him to ask why. What he told me made me proud of the NCOs who preceded me and left me profoundly aware of my duty to make every action I undertook as an NCO confirm the validity of his belief.

He said, "… if we are envied, admired, or feared by military forces around the world, it is not because we have officers who've graduated academies or because we have people with advanced academic degrees. It is because of our NCO Corps." This was a General officer declaring our NCO Corps the foundation of our service's global reputation as planet Earth's preeminent Air Force. Wow! Of course, now I needed to know more; I needed to know why he believed this.

"Trust and culture", he said. "The NCO Corps has earned the trust of its senior leaders through years of proven performance. I've seen a single NCO deliver mission success

---

[1] Noncommissioned Officer (NCO) in the United States Air Force (USAF) describes the middle tier (E5/E6) of enlisted ranks; according to USAF Instruction 36-2618, NCOs lead and develop subordinates, exercise effective followership in mission accomplishment, and place requirements of official duties and responsibilities ahead of personal desires

by articulating his leader's guidance and intent in terms every Airman could clearly understand and act upon at the tactical level. As a young officer, I quickly learned my NCOs were not only trained (what to think) to be technically proficient, but had attained education (how to think) levels never before seen by any military's enlisted force, providing them the critical capability to improvise, adapt, and innovate in any situation. I learned NCOs are our standard bearers; not only knowing the standards, but also grasping the necessity to communicate to our entire force how compliance with standards directly impacts mission accomplishment. In fact, our best NCOs ensure everyone knows two things about them; what they stand for and what they will not tolerate."

"The NCO Corps also understands how culture can shape Airmen of all grades. Our NCOs have fostered a culture embracing governance by a set of values and principles considered more important and enduring than any individual. Our NCOs have built a disciplined apprenticeship process, insisting everything be done the right way, for the right reasons, even during times when no one else is watching. This disciplined apprenticeship also supports a culture where all practice and teach loyalty to the chain of command, helping all to understand their 'lane in the road'; helping all to learn when to speak up, and when after speaking up to know when it's time to go back to work, trusting leaders to work the issue."

He added, "… trust and culture require deliberate and continuous effort to maintain. Beware of their fragility."

Sir Winston Churchill said, "To build may have to be the slow and laborious task of years. To destroy can be the thoughtless act of a single day."

The General finished up with, "encourage our NCOs to be aware how their actions can further solidify the global reputation of the NCO Corps; caution them to be aware how their actions can damage the trust and culture upon which this reputation is based."

To say I was glad I approached the General after his remarks that evening many years ago would be an understatement. I walked away that evening committed to always working hard to gain and preserve my leader's trust and I've challenged myself and my NCOs to further cement our culture of disciplined adherence to standards. It is on each of us to ensure "the NCO Corps is the backbone of the Air Force" remains a quote that rings true with all who are within earshot wherever and whenever it may be spoken.

You Get What You Tolerate

If you've served in the military for any length of time, you've undoubtedly spent quite a few hours of your life standing in formation during open ranks inspections, changes-of-command, retirement parades, or other formal military ceremonies. I'm also sure you've seen people fall out, some on their faces and others pulled out of formation at the first sign of distress.

As a young NCO, following an opportunity to stand in a change-of-command formation one afternoon, I asked my supervisor his thoughts on why people seemed to be falling out earlier and earlier (some didn't even make it to the invocation—the invocation was barely five minutes into the ceremony) and in greater numbers (I think we lost five people from a fifty-person formation that day). He delivered a very short response. "You get what you tolerate", he said.

"Tolerate?" I asked. "Nobody appears to be happy about it or even ok with it. What do you mean by tolerate?" He looked more than a little irritated when he gave me his full explanation.

He said, "Before every opportunity we remind everyone to hydrate, to wiggle their toes, to bounce slightly on the balls of their feet, not to lock their knees, and not to focus their vision on a single object or point. Yet, every time we have at least a few people fail to follow our direction and fall out. How do we respond? We respond by having First

14

Sergeants, supervisors, medics and others coddle them, console them, and fawn over them. We darn near feel bad for them. I can't think of another task we charge our people to carry out where we respond to failure in this way."

He went on to say, "Think about it. Even our language encourages this behavior. During the planning meeting, do planners say, let's have First Sergeants and medics ready *just in case* people fall out? Of course not. They say, let's have first sergeants and medics ready for *WHEN* people fall out. Geez, we even have 'extras' often placed behind the formation to 'fill in the hole' NOT in case someone falls out, but for WHEN someone falls out. We've planned a self-fulfilling prophecy. We're telling our Airmen we expect them to fall out rather than telling our Airmen it is unacceptable to fall out."

He finished with, "Have you ever wondered why the commander of troops, Group, Squadron, or Flight Commander, First Sergeant, flag and/or guidon bearer never fall out, yet any number of flight members do? Not one of these primary players in a formation would ever bring upon themselves the embarrassment of falling out in full view of participants and guests. The self-discipline instilled in each serves as all the motivation they need to remain standing tall even while their feet tire and sweat brings discomfort to places we won't discuss. They wouldn't tolerate themselves falling out."

Want to stop the madness? Tell your people you won't tolerate them falling out of formation. Consider reprimanding those who do. Think that's too harsh? Well, then you'll continue to get what you tolerate—and you can bet these results will extend beyond formations too—it's just a matter of time. What else will you tolerate?

<u>Remedial Training</u>

While assigned to a joint-service communications station earlier in my career, I learned a lot about effective tactical-level leadership (frontline supervision) from the soldiers, sailors, and Marines on my team. In fact, a lesson in remedial training ranks right up there with the most valuable leadership lessons I've learned.

One day, I witnessed Army Sergeant (SGT) Ortega (E-5/squad leader) correct a soldier for failing to maintain Army standards. I was sitting at my desk (my desk faced SGT Ortega's) when a disheveled Private First Class (PFC/E-3) approached and came to the position of attention. I barely noticed the PFC, but when SGT Ortega starting speaking to him, I found myself in full 'eavesdrop mode'. I was about to get an 'everything you ever needed to know about the need for, and the effectiveness of, remedial training' lesson and I was going to get it from a master.

"Soldier," said SGT Ortega in a cool, calm, and collected voice. "I wish to apologize." What? An Army NCO apologizing to a soldier? I was definitely paying close attention at this point (in fact, I couldn't believe my ears). "I have obviously failed to properly train you. And, for this, I apologize. My failure has apparently resulted in you believing Army Regulations allow you to wear a uniform that's been dragged out from under your bed or dug up from the bottom

17

of your laundry bag." The PFC, at the position of attention, didn't say a word. Good move.

"So," said SGT Ortega. "While our squad is preparing to go off duty for the next three days (we'd just completed our third 12-hour shift of a three-on/three-off schedule), your understanding of Army standards is going to delay the two of us; me for one hour and you for 13." This was definitely getting interesting. "You and I will review Army Regulation 670-1, *Wear and Appearance of Army Uniforms and Insignia*[2] for the next hour. Then, I will begin my three-day break. To ensure you've learned and can meet the expected standard you will then perform the following task":

"For the next 12 hours, you will report to SGT Croft (the squad leader coming on duty) at this desk, every hour, on the hour in a different uniform combination, ready for inspection. Following each inspection, SGT Croft will instruct you as to which uniform combination you'll be required to wear for the next hour's inspection."

Wow, I thought to myself. For showing to duty in a sloppy uniform this soldier was going to spend his off-duty time running back and forth to/from his barracks to report to the squad leader on duty every hour, on the hour in a different uniform combination for the next 12 hours. Wow!

---

[2] AR 670-1 can be found at
http://www.apd.army.mil/pdffiles/r670_1.pdf

Old School is Good School

Some of you may think SGT Ortega was being cruel or unnecessarily harsh, but I disagree. In my mind, SGT Ortega's response was a thing of beauty. Why?

1. He was swift (no one was going to talk ad nauseam about what to do—it was handled immediately)

2. He did it at his level (SGT Ortega had NCO authority/responsibility—he didn't ask someone to tell him what to do, he knew what to do, and he did it)

3. He trained, he did not punish (he retrained and reinforced to ensure learning occurred—he didn't have his soldier doing push-ups for having a sloppy uniform—that would have been punishment (NCOs don't punish, commanders do) and pointless (what do push-ups have to do with a sloppy uniform?))

4. He never mentioned LOC, LOR, or any other paper as a solution (he'd undoubtedly document the entire incident, but he'd never suggest an LOC, LOR, or other paper was the solution—it's just paper)[3]

---

[3] Simply issuing a letter of counseling (LOC) or letter of reprimand (LOR) accomplishes nothing; take ACTION and then document the ACTION in an LOC or LOR

5. He knew this was the end of it (you think any soldier in his squad—or once word got out—in any other squad, ever wore a sloppy uniform, showed up late, or failed to meet any other established standard?)

By the way, remedial training is not just for uniform violations. I've seen its effective application in response to showing up late, parking tickets, and seat belt violations. Remedial training is also not an Army thing. It's an NCO thing. In fact, holding your subordinates accountable when they do not meet established standards is a general NCO responsibility levied on you by the Air Force—it's right there in paragraph 4.1.10 of Air Force Instruction 36-2618, The Enlisted Force Structure (27 Feb 09).[4]

---

[4] You can find the Air Force's Enlisted Force Structure at http://www.e-publishing.af.mil/shared/media/epubs/AFI36-2618.pdf

Bones

The human body's 206 bones serve to strengthen our skeleton, to protect internal organs, and to provide a place for muscles to attach. But is every bone vital? Which ones are most important? While I won't add to the debate on the relative value of each and every bone to each and every person, I do believe the three most important bones in a leader's body are the funny bone, the backbone, and the wishbone.

The leader with a funny bone takes only the serious seriously and never himself too seriously. He easily distinguishes hiccups from crises and ensures his Airmen can too. The leader with a funny bone knows how to use humor to connect with his Airmen, to break the ice, to ease any tension, and to help his Airmen and his organization through tough times.

The leader with a backbone stands for something. He doesn't just 'talk the talk' but firmly 'walks the talk', understanding his actions will always speak louder than his words. The leader with a backbone embraces the standard, explains the standard to his Airmen, and then holds his Airmen (of all grades) to the standard. The leader with a backbone recognizes mission accomplishment hinges heavily on responsible and accountable Airmen—this is why he will not tolerate any Airman failing to meet the standard.

The leader with a wishbone dreams, wonders, and asks the questions 'what if', 'why not', and 'how come'. By doing

21

so, he builds Airmen who will do the same, focusing not only on how to get the mission done, but how to get it done better. The leader with a wishbone builds Airmen, who while implementing today's tactics, techniques, and procedures, are constantly probing, questioning, and examining our methods for even the smallest improvement opportunities. The leader with a wishbone respects today's way of doing business, but also encourages his unit to invest time and energy into how to do our mission better tomorrow.

Each day when I drag my 206 bones out of bed I always take time to check the status of my critical three: my funny bone, my backbone, and my wishbone. As long as these are intact, I'm good to go.

Expectation Not Reward

"Congratulations Staff Sergeant (SSgt) Slater, you've been selected for promotion to Technical Sergeant[5] (TSgt)."

I have vivid memories of my commander visiting me to deliver this message in the Operations Training office at Royal Air Force Chicksands, England many years ago. Man, was I stoked; selected to TSgt with just six years in service. To be honest, humility took a serious backseat at that moment. I thought I was the man! Fortunately, I had a supervisor who knew better. As soon as the commander left, my supervisor invited me to step outside for a mentoring moment.

I'll never forget what he told me that day.

"Kevin, congratulations on your selection … you've earned it and I'm proud of you. Now, I want you to go home and thank your wife for the sacrifices she made by allowing you to trade family time for study time (he knew I'd been studying many hours after duty and on weekends for many months)—you couldn't have done this without her. Then we'll see you at the club this afternoon where the entire base will 'tip one' in your honor on 'your dime' (his way of reminding me to bring money to put on the bar—an act I had zero heartburn with performing—it was the most appropriate way to thank my teammates for the constant support they'd given me)."

---

[5] Staff Sergeant (SSgt) and Technical Sergeant (TSgt) are the Air Force's two NCO grades

He continued, "Before you go, I just want to be sure you understand *exactly* what you've earned today." Understand what I'd earned? Of course I understood. I'd earned promotion to Technical Sergeant, a reward for my knowledge, skill, and performance. I didn't know it at the time, but I wasn't as smart as I thought I was. Fortunately, my supervisor wasn't going to allow me to remain dumb for long.

He shook his head, "Kevin, your promotion isn't a reward. It's an expectation." What? An expectation? Not a reward? Once again my supervisor was speaking a language he and I did not share (this happened often). In fact, people often ask me if learning to speak Russian was difficult. I usually respond, "yes, but not nearly as difficult as learning to speak Supervisor."

"Kevin, your promotion isn't a reward for yesterday's knowledge, skill, or performance. It is an expectation that you will fulfill your potential to perform tomorrow's broader set of tasks to an ever-increasing standard. Should you feel good about your selection? Absolutely! I just don't want you to mistake the Air Force's motives. The Air Force didn't promote you because you *are* awesome. They promoted you because they expect you to **become** awesome, rising to meet the challenges sure to come with the responsibilities and authorities of your next grade."

I've carried this mentoring moment with me ever since. Promotion isn't a reward for past performance. It's an expectation of future performance. Confusing the two could prove disastrous for my Airmen and my organization. If I thought it was a reward for past performance, I may have been tempted to take the promotion, to consider me and the Air Force even, and to rest on my laurels. I may have thought I no longer owed my subordinates and superiors the best I had to offer. I'm glad my supervisor set me straight, because I wouldn't want someone with that attitude on my team, would you?

Give 'em HELL

During a speech given by Harry Truman in the 1948 Presidential election campaign an animated supporter in the crowd yelled, "give 'em hell, Harry!" This fiery shout of support stuck with Harry Truman for the remainder of the campaign, became a lifetime slogan for his supporters, and later served as the title of a biographical play and film about the former President.

I bet if Harry Truman were serving in our Air Force today he'd tell us all to get out there and "give our people hell," as in **H**onesty, **E**ffort, **L**oyalty, and **L**eadership.

Without honesty we cannot have trust. Trust is the backbone of every successful relationship and without relationships we don't have teamwork. No honesty = no trust = no relationships = no teamwork = mission failure. I believe we owe it to each other to tell it like it is. Honest feedback, honest assessments, and honest answers will enable trust and build stronger teams, improving the likelihood of mission accomplishment.

While we can't control which talents or abilities we're born with, we can control a key ingredient in our ability to succeed—effort. I'm convinced mission accomplishment hinges heavily upon the willingness of every Airman to give maximum effort. I've been given assignments, jobs, and duty schedules that didn't thrill me. But, I bet none of my leaders could ever tell by my effort. I have always responded in every circumstance with the one thing under my total control, my best effort. It is essential we each respond even in less-than-perfect circumstances with maximum effort and expect the same from our teammates.

Have you ever worked in an organization poisoned by people who support you when talking to you face-to-face, but undermine your efforts once you've turned your back? Without loyalty our organization crumbles and our mission fails. I will ask questions and provide constructive criticism when I disagree or don't understand, but I will always take ownership of my leader's decision once the final call has been made. This is called loyalty. We must all possess it, encourage it in others, and admonish those in whom it is absent.

Effective leadership will fuel an Airman's desire to perform. What fuel should the leader use? Belief! Airmen will outperform their own expectations if they're fueled by their leader's belief in their ability to succeed. In those moments throughout my career when I may have lacked confidence in myself it was my leader's belief in me that inspired me to succeed. Our leadership challenge is to establish a climate of high expectations, 'to set the bar' high and to support our Airmen by teaching each of them to believe in themselves.

What's my bottom line? The best leaders don't 'baby', 'coddle', or 'hand-hold'. The best leaders give their people HELL everyday; **H**onesty, **E**ffort, **L**oyalty, and **L**eadership.

27

I've Got Your Back

I had just crossed the stage after receiving my NCO Preparatory Course completion certificate when my supervisor approached, shook my hand, and said, "I've got your back." I nodded and walked back to my seat. As I sat there clapping my hands in support of my fellow graduates, I began to think about what my supervisor had said only moments ago, "I've got your back". What did she mean by that? Was someone out to get me? I was expecting a pat on the back, not a cryptic comment regarding my personal safety.

My supervisor sometimes delivered leadership messages to me in obscure comments or cryptic words of advice. Well, this case was no different. I had just completed the Air Force's required course for Airmen wishing to become supervisors for the first time (Airmen today complete Airman Leadership School to earn this privilege) and my supervisor didn't step up to say 'good job', 'well done', or 'I'm proud of you'. Instead, she had me wondering what on Earth she was talking about with 'I've got your back'.

When I arrived for duty the following day, I immediately asked my supervisor if I could have a moment of her time. Fortunately this was something she gave me anytime I asked. As I pulled my chair up beside her I asked, "What did you mean yesterday when you said 'I've got your back'?" Her response was unexpected and enlightening. "Kevin, everyone has a specific role to play on our team. Prior to today, your

28

role has been to focus solely on yourself; to master the skills required of every Airman. My role has been to help you get there. As of today, your role has changed. You are now a frontline supervisor and will add 'responsibility for others' to your job jar. My role has also changed. I'm now your first line of defense. So, I've got your back."

"What do I mean by this? When requirements and tasks flow downhill from those above us, I've got your back. I'll ensure our leadership is always aware of the requirements you and your Airmen are already working. I'll also ensure the tasks you and your Airmen are working are appropriately prioritized, so you never have to worry about risking mission failure by working the wrong (lowest priority) tasks."

"More importantly, as a supervisor you'll be asked to make many decisions affecting the personal and professional lives of your Airmen (duty schedules, training requirements, details, etc). Trust me, when you make a decision your Airmen don't agree with they're going to come to me to complain about it. When this happens, you need to know I've got your back."

"I won't throw you under the bus. I will never question your decisions in front of your Airmen. In fact, I'll always support your decision (even if I don't agree with it). More importantly, I'll never ask you to change a decision you've made as long as the decision is not illegal, immoral, or unethical. You AND your Airmen need to know YOU are the decision-maker and you have authority commensurate with your responsibility (these two must always go hand-in-hand)."

I'll never forget this conversation. Throughout the years, all of my experiences as an NCO and a supervisor have proven her right. I needed something more than congratulations that day. I needed to know she had my back. In fact, her support gave me the confidence to perform right out of the blocks. To this day, I support every supervisor by assuring them, "I've got your back."

The Least We Can Do

Throughout my career, I've witnessed leaders at every level consistently deliver an expectation that every member of our team give everything they've got to every assigned task. Knowing this, I wonder if the title of this story seems as odd to you as it did to me when I first wrote it. 'The least we can do'? When did 'least' enter our lexicon? Allow me to explain.

Quite a few years ago, in 1989 to be exact, I was a young NCO weaving my way in line behind our squadron superintendent (a Chief Master Sergeant) preparing to congratulate a Master Sergeant (MSgt) from our unit upon his retirement (his ceremony had ended just moments before).

If you've read this far into the book, you know throughout my career I've described being in the right place at the right time to receive valuable leadership lessons. You also know, while each lesson was very different, my role in each was exactly the same -- pay very close attention to ensure the lesson was learned and not just observed (big difference between the two).

As the Chief approached to shake the hand of our retiree, I heard the MSgt say, "Chief, I can never thank you enough for making me do this." I paused, digested what I'd just overheard, continued to congratulate family members and our MSgt, and then made a bee-line directly for the Chief. "Chief, I heard him thank you for making him do this. What did he mean by that? Why did our MSgt thank you for making him retire?"

The Chief replied, "SSgt Slater, he wasn't thanking me for making him retire. He was thanking me for insisting he allow us to organize a retirement ceremony. Throughout my career, I've seen some of our most dedicated members ask not to have a ceremony. At first I thought they were angry at the Air Force, bitter about the conclusion of their service, or indifferent about their accomplishments. But I was wrong. I quickly learned almost all of them were neither fans of the limelight (preferred to shine the light on anyone but themselves) nor interested in putting people out (all understood the amount of work it takes to put on an appropriate retirement ceremony). I also learned I'd be disappointed in any organization that would so easily allow a member who'd invested at least two decades of blood, sweat, and tears into the success of the organization to simply walk away without as much as a thank you."

He continued, "Today's retiree thanked me just as nearly every other NCO and SNCO[6] who initially balked has done following their ceremonies. Why do I think he was thankful? When he saw a room full of proud teammates, his

---

[6] Senior Noncommissioned Officer (SNCO) in the United States Air Force (USAF) describes the highest tier (E7-E9) of enlisted ranks; according to USAF Instruction 36-2618, a SNCO's primary responsibility is mission accomplishment; leading and managing teams while maintaining the highest levels of readiness to ensure mission success

family front and center, and the disciplined performance of emcees, proffers, Honor Guard members, and flag bearers he got a visual of the definition of 'what is right'."

The Chief admitted to me he'd 'leaned' on many a retiring member to allow his unit to organize a retirement ceremony. But, he also admitted he'd yet to shake the hand of a retiring member unhappy about being thanked for their faithful service or unhappy witnessing his family finally being recognized for the birthdays, anniversaries, and other special moments sacrificed in favor of TDYs[7], remotes[8], and deployments or unhappy that the Airmen succeeding him had the opportunity to learn how sometimes 'the least you can do' is also the right thing to do.

What did I learn that day? Retiring soon? Congratulations! Don't 'want' a ceremony? No problem. You don't have to 'want' one. I'd insist you have one anyway. In fact, "It's the least we can do"!

---

[7] TDY – Temporary Duty – Normally a duty performed for less than 179 days away from your permanent duty location
[8] A remote assignment is an assignment to a location which prohibits family members from accompanying the member

Cato Leads The Way

As I was preparing to leave the 480th Intelligence Wing to serve a year-long deployment to Southwest Asia, Technical Sergeant Lucrica 'Cato' Gilliam[9] and I had a conversation about the duties and responsibilities she should seek as her career progressed. Her time serving as the assistant to the Command Chief would soon come to an end and Cato was interested in what I thought she ought to do next.

I told her the specific duty didn't matter—I knew she would be a superior performer in whatever duty position the Air Force assigned her. What really mattered was to have responsibility for people—she needed to be a supervisor of Airmen and Noncommissioned Officers to build her competency as a leader.

I left for Southwest Asia and Cato later moved to a communications-computer operations floor as a section supervisor where she had responsibility for Airmen. Perfect!

On my return to Langley Air Force Base a year later, my first phone call was from Cato. "Chief, we need to meet for lunch", she said. She wanted to fill me in on her experiences as a supervisor over the past year.

"Chief, this supervision and leadership stuff has been hard—I mean really hard—people sure can be a challenge."

---

[9] Cato served as the assistant to the Command Chief Master Sergeant, 480th Intelligence Wing in 2007; I'll share the story behind her nickname some other time

Then her face lit up as she began to describe the day she learned her commander respected her position as a leader in her organization. She had been summoned to the commander's office to discuss a disciplinary issue involving one of her Airmen. She expected the commander to express his dissatisfaction with the Airman's behavior and maybe even with her leadership performance (she expected to be blamed for her Airman's behavior).

In fact, the conversation in the commander's office was 180 degrees out from what she had imagined. When she entered the commander's office, he asked her one very simple question. He said, "so Cato, what do you think?" She thought, what do I think? Instead of being blamed for the Airman's behavior, she was being asked for her professional opinion on whether this Airman could be rehabilitated and how unit leadership should respond to secure a change in this Airman's behavior. All she could think as she exited the office was "wow, my opinion matters." This episode stuck with her and ultimately made a difference in how she supported her Airmen in the future.

One day, Cato was supporting one of her Airmen completing his annual physical fitness test (part of the test is a timed 1 ½ mile run—six laps around a standard ¼ mile track) when she saw the Airman come around the final bend on his fifth lap. When the test proctor shouted out the lap time, the Airman began to walk. It appeared he'd realized that his time at the conclusion of the fifth lap was so poor that no matter how quickly he ran the sixth lap his overall time would be too slow to pass the test. "Chief", she said, "I had an instantaneous out-of-body experience. The next thing I know I'm on the track; chasing him; screaming 'encouragement'[10] for him to RUN the sixth and final lap."

At the conclusion of the run, Cato was careful to explain to the Airman what had just happened. "Why do you think I chased after you?" she asked.

"You were angry with me for walking?" he replied.

"Yes. I mean no. I mean, sure I was angry to see you walking. But, more importantly, when I saw you walking I could see myself in the commander's office tomorrow talking with him about your physical fitness test failure. I know he has a range of disciplinary options available to him (verbal counseling to written admonition/reprimand) and he'll want to know what I think before he acts. When I saw you walking all I could hear in my head was the commander asking, "so, Cato what do you think"?"

"I knew if you had walked the final lap your score would likely have been around 55 (75 is a passing score), and how I would have answered his question would be radically different than how I'll answer his question now that you've run

---

[10] Encouragement in this instance was in the form of a few choice words I know Cato not only never used in the office, but likely had never used before in her entire life

the last lap and scored a 70 (still failing, but at least not quitting)."

What I learned from Cato over lunch that day was her leadership skills had matured dramatically in one year. She not only learned her commander respected her opinion as a frontline supervisor, but she understood the need to articulate her leadership responsibilities to her Airmen in order to gain their trust.

It should come as no surprise that this Airman later returned to the track in the minimum time allowed for retesting and knocked out a passing score. Some may suggest his fitness had improved in this short period of time allowing him to run faster. I suggest he ran better not only for himself that day, but for the supervisor he knew cared about him. By the way, care doesn't mean coddle. It means willing to show your Airman you're not ready to quit on them even when they appear ready to quit on themselves.

Be the Good Boss

Each year, thousands of Airmen are selected for promotion to Staff Sergeant and offered the opportunity to attend Airman Leadership School in order to prepare for the significant life-altering event of becoming a supervisor for the very first time. I remember when I had my first shot at being a supervisor. I desperately wanted to be the good boss, mimicking all the best actions of my best supervisors and vowing not to copy any of the worst actions of my worst supervisors. Recently, one of my mentors (yes, even Chiefs have mentors) sent me an article he came across outlining good boss/bad boss behaviors. The author of the article, Martha Beck[11], does a great job of highlighting the damage faulty logic can have on one's performance as a boss. Here are some of the highlights:

Bad boss: Now that I'm in charge, I can give orders
Good boss: Now that I'm in charge, I bring order to what my people do

Bad boss: Now everyone has to tell me that I'm right
Good boss: Now I must make it acceptable for everyone to tell me when I'm wrong

---

[11] Martha Beck, Ph.D., author and life coach holds three social-science degrees from Harvard University and is also a monthly columnist for O, The Oprah Magazine

Bad boss: As the boss, I'll be protected from blame
Good boss: As the boss, I'll protect others by taking the blame

Some of our very best people get sidetracked on their journey to becoming the good boss. Many misunderstand the target audience—they think it's all about them when it's not about them at all. It's about our mission and the people who accomplish it—the people we lead.

The good boss supports our people not only when they succeed, but also when they fail. They deliver more vision than orders and create an environment where everyone is comfortable saying what they think, especially when their thoughts differ from those of others. The good boss is not focused on their own position or duty title. They're focused on the professional and personal development of our people with goals of creating fine Airmen and fine citizens.

By willingly supporting Airmen following success or failure, by delivering vision more than orders, by encouraging all sides in a debate, and by focusing more on the development of their people than on themselves, our Air Force's newest supervisors are sure to have a positive impact on mission accomplishment. I always look forward to seeing them in action!

My Two Favorite Questions

I've often wondered how many things I might have done differently as a young supervisor if I'd known then what I know now. One thing is for sure, I would have definitely reacted differently to some of the questions my Airmen were asking me. In fact, two questions I wish I was better at answering back then are now my favorite questions to be asked; my two favorite questions? 'Why' and 'How Come'.

As a first-time supervisor and inexperienced leader, I completely misunderstood these two questions. I thought *'why'* and *'how come'* were indicators of whining Airmen rather than of Airmen interested in better understanding the data, background, or intent behind a decision. I wasn't equipped yet to understand that our most invested Airmen ask 'why' or 'how come' as a way of exhibiting strong followership behavior. My Airmen needed to know 'why' or 'how come' in order to provide timely, constructive feedback to me, to take responsibility for supporting the decision, and to effectively explain the decision to their subordinates and peers.

I completely misunderstood the opportunity my Airmen were giving me when asking me these two great questions. By misinterpreting these questions as noise or nuisance, I didn't clearly see then what I now understand as the two guaranteed benefits answering these questions is sure to deliver. I was either going to gain Airmen more committed to the decision by taking the time to help them to better

40

understand it or I was going to realize my decision might need adjustments if/when I found myself unable to adequately explain 'why' or 'how come'.

I know I've learned many leadership lessons over the years as I've grown from a young, first-time supervisor to a seasoned Chief Master Sergeant. One of my most important lessons learned is "listen to our people, especially when they ask questions." Our people will provide us with all we need to make the best decisions for our unit and for our Air Force if we create an environment which encourages them to ask my two favorite questions, 'why' and 'how come'.

A Little More Than Duty

Unfortunately, we've all seen huddled masses in doorways moments before retreat[12] is played; so many people engaged in a disappointing and disrespectful internal debate—do I stay here (pretending I don't hear the music play) or sprint to my car before the music starts?

I think you'll find screaming and hollering at good, yet misguided people is often ineffective and frustrating for both parties involved. In fact, when I come across people engaged in strange behaviors in order to avoid being 'caught' outdoors during retreat, I slip them a copy of this poem a friend shared with me many years ago—I then walk away without saying a word. I can tell the message has gotten through just by the look on their face as they finish reading. Go ahead, print a few copies on cards and pass them out. Your encouragement will no doubt assist our Airmen (of all grades) in learning why it's so important to perform a little more than duty.

---

[12] Airmen signal the end of every duty day by lowering our flag to the sound of our National Anthem. While the flag is lowered and the national anthem played, vehicles are expected to stop, occupants are expected to sit quietly, and Airmen outdoors are to stand at the position of 'attention' and render a hand salute (unfortunately, some see this opportunity to honor our nation's most recognizable symbol as a chore rather than a tribute to be performed)

Old School is Good School

Somewhere a bugle sounds
And men inside their building wait
Until the flag comes down.

And others run to get to their car
Quite harrowed or dismayed
Afraid they will not reach the gate
Before "Retreat is played".

Not thinking of the flag or men
Who fought to keep it flying.
How many would be glad to stand
Whose bodies now are mute.
Or have no hand
That they might raise
And stand in proud salute.

So accept it not as duty,
But a privilege even more.
And receive it as an honor,
Instead of just a chore.

Author unknown

My professional duties take precedence over my personal desires.

Chapter 2

SERVICE-BEFORE-SELF

I have the self-discipline to place the needs of my Airmen and my organization above my own.

<u>Followership</u>

I bet we'd agree even the best leaders accomplish nothing without effective followers. If we agree followers are essential, why do so many people take being called a good follower as a criticism rather than as a compliment?

I'm looking at the word leadership in the dictionary right now. It has many definitions and each one paints a picture of strength. Yet I can't find 'followership' in the dictionary at all. It appears to be 'Rodney Dangerfield'[1] in the leader-follower relationship—"it gets no respect".

Why should followership get more respect? If we don't learn and practice effective followership skills, we're destined to fail our leaders and ultimately negatively impact our mission.

Why do I believe the best follower is at least as valuable as the best leader? The best follower displays initiative, provides constructive criticism, asks thought-provoking questions to gain clarification, and accepts responsibility and accountability for results. The best follower also brings solutions, or at least proposed courses of action, whenever he brings challenges to the leader. Finally, agree or disagree, once the leader considers the follower's feedback and

---

[1] Rodney Dangerfield (born Jacob Cohen, 22 Nov 1921 – 5 Oct 2004) was an American comedian known for the catchphrases "I don't get no respect!," "No respect, no respect at all... that's the story of my life" or "I get no respect, I tell ya" and his monologues on that theme

makes a decision, the best follower takes ownership of the decision and champions the decision throughout the organization as if it were his own. This is called loyalty and it must live inside every follower.

I bet many of you think fulfilling my responsibilities as a Numbered Air Force Command Chief takes well-honed leadership skills. Would you be surprised if I told you it takes even better-honed followership skills?

I gauge my strength as a follower by the answers I give to these six questions. Feel free to use these questions to gauge your followership skills. Would you and your leader be happy with your answers?

1. Do I know and understand what my leader expects of me?

2. Have I earned my leader's trust by displaying my loyalty?

3. Do I present solutions or courses of action when I present challenges?

4. Do I provide relevant and timely information to my leader before he makes decisions?

5. Do I champion my leader's decisions throughout my organization as if they were my own?

6. If I disagree with a decision do I champion in public and critique respectfully in private?

I'm proud to be a senior enlisted leader in the United States Air Force, but more importantly I'm proud to be a follower of the many great leaders in our organization! I am proud of my role as a follower. It does not make me weak. It makes me and my organization strong!

Commitment

I met an NCO today with orders for a 12-month remote to Korea. Yes, that's right, 12 months unaccompanied. We talked for a while about some of the hardships an unaccompanied tour may bring. We talked about what it's like to be geographically removed from day-to-day participation in the lives of your loved ones. We also agreed e-mail, web cameras, and telephone calls may help, but they will never remove the sting of family separation.

Is she the first NCO to have to go through this? No. Is she going to be the last? No. Should we cry for her and her circumstances? No. Should we applaud her commitment? Absolutely! Could she have a "woe is me" attitude? Yes. Does she? Heck no! Why not?

This NCO is a professional Airman in the United States Air Force. Her voluntary service to her nation requires her commitment to duty and subordination to our Air Force core values: Integrity First, Service-Before-Self, and Excellence In All We Do.

What does all this mean? It means she knows the only thing for her to do is to sacrifice, to remain committed, and to place service before self. If she didn't believe this to be true, I'm sure she wouldn't have enlisted and most definitely would

48

not have reenlisted[2] a short time ago. She signed up to a commitment and is prepared to uphold her end of the bargain.

I believe this NCO views her assignment as yet another opportunity to exercise 'servant leadership'. She's not about to ask someone to help her to get out of this assignment nor is she contemplating getting out of the Air Force simply because she received orders to Korea. She chose to serve her country and right now her country needs her in Korea.

I'm proud of this NCO and her attitude. At a time in her life when it might be very easy for her to find many reasons not to remain committed, she's instead prepared to stay the course, to fulfill her commitment, and to honor our Air Force Core Values. She's stepped up to the plate and hit a Home Run--like so many American Airmen do!

---

[2] An enlistment is an enlisted person's initial contract to serve. A reenlistment describes each subsequent contract to continue to serve; always voluntary and normally in four to six year increments

Travel in Uniform

Prior to the attacks of 9/11, senior leaders across our Air Force were encouraging Airmen to wear a blue uniform when traveling on orders across our country on commercial aircraft. In fact, I remember carrying a few extra neckties in my bag in case I came across an Airmen who'd forgotten to wear a tie (ties were required for travel at the time).

Immediately after 9/11, wearing our uniform in public was seen by some as a force protection risk and our Airmen were encouraged to stop wearing their uniform in public. I believe this sent an unbelievably negative message to our Airmen and to the American public. "It's dangerous out there, so we're going to ask our fully trained warriors, your sentries and avengers, to not wear their uniforms in public." Our country needed a confidence boost ... it NEEDED to see its military personnel. One could argue a better idea at the time may have been for uniform wear to be mandated for all official travel as a show of force.

In 2008, our Air Force leadership made a remarkably positive decision to not only encourage our Airmen to wear their uniform when traveling on orders, but to allow Airmen for the first time in our history to wear Airman Battle Uniforms (ABU) when traveling on orders. This sent an awesome message to our Airmen (take pride in your uniform, and not just your blues) and to the American public (we are your Airmen, we are your warriors, we have answered your call).

"Excuse me sir. I'm on my way to San Antonio to watch my grandson's basic training graduation parade on Friday. Can you tell me what time the parade begins?"

"Excuse me Sergeant. I retired from the Air Force almost 20 years ago. I don't recognize the stripes you're wearing--three stripes on top and a solid star in the field of blue. What is your rank?"

"Excuse me Chief. Where are you stationed? My brother is in the Air Force. Maybe you know him?"

What do these questions, and the many others posed to me in airports around the country, have in common? None would have been posed to me had I not been traveling in uniform. No one would have approached me with their question about basic training, our stripes, or our people if I'd not appropriately understood and responded to my leadership's encouragement to wear my uniform when traveling on orders.

Next time you're handed travel orders, please don't let internal arguments of inconvenience talk you out of traveling in uniform. Wearing our uniform proudly when traveling on orders sends the right message to the American public and to our adversaries. We want the public to see us, to approach us, to learn about us, to know they can count on us. And we want

51

our adversaries to know we've no intention to hide from them; we plan to be visible guardians of freedom and justice.

Professional Courtesy

As a Senior Airman in England in 1987, I saw an article in the base paper advertising for Russian linguists to serve at the U.S. Embassy in Moscow. At the height of the Cold War, this looked like the opportunity of a lifetime. I went home and asked my wife what she thought of **us** volunteering. I use the word '**us**' purposely. Our wedding vows cemented our relationship as a team. I knew I had no right to volunteer for something without her being on board.

I went in for a weekend mid shift the following night and told my co-workers about my plan to volunteer as soon as Monday morning rolled around (no cool electronic, computer tools in those days to communicate my wishes). I needed to wait until Monday so I could make a phone call to the office owning the program.

I was pretty excited about my plan until one of the NCOs on my flight overheard me. I was quite surprised at first by what he said to me. "There's no Air Force policy which says you have to get your supervisor's permission, but you should still tell your supervisor what you're planning to do before you do it. It's a professional courtesy, in fact a professional obligation."

Of course, I coughed up the typical "why the heck would I want to do that" response. I really didn't understand why I should have to tell my supervisor anything about my plan. It didn't affect him. He wasn't going to Moscow. I was (or at least I hoped I was).

I didn't understand this NCO's point at all, so he explained further, "If you're selected, your supervisor will have to modify training plans, work assignments, and duty schedules. And then, oh yeah, who do you think will be working the phones to identify a replacement for you?" I began to realize my supervisor deserved a heads up. I also understood this wasn't an attempt by my leadership to mess with my plan. They simply needed to know about it. It all sounded reasonable now. Permission wasn't what I was seeking nor was it what was being offered.

Thanks to this NCO taking the time to explain it to me rather than just telling me what I was going to do because it was 'mandatory', I understood my commitment to my unit, my flight, and my supervisor. Just as I had no right to volunteer '**us**' (my home team) without speaking to my wife, I also owed it to my supervisor (my Air Force team) to let him know my plan.

When I did tell my supervisor my plan that night he actually thanked me. He appreciated the heads up. He even offered to help me clear hurdles should any pop up during the application process. I learned a lot that night about professional courtesy and its impact on the team. My supervisor had a job to do (many in fact) and giving him the courtesy of a heads up prepared him for what could lie ahead, which in turn kept the entire team on track.

Do you have your eye on that choice training opportunity or assignment? Great! Good luck. I hope you get what you're looking for. But first, please extend some professional courtesy and tell your supervisor your plans.

Put Me In Coach

In earlier stories, I've introduced you to some of the cryptic responses I used to get from my supervisor when I'd ask questions as an Airman. As soon as he started talking about windshields, rear view mirrors, or walls that weren't walls my eyes would glaze over. Of course, he'd eventually get around to translating his comments for me and then I'd be good-to-go. I'm convinced he enjoyed the twisted journey we'd travel from question to whacky response, to odd look on my face, to translation, to eventual comprehension. Knowing this, it will come as no surprise that his response to a question I asked during a career counseling session left me dumbfounded.

There I was, sitting with him during a mandatory career counseling session, when I asked, "what will it take for me to get ahead, for me to have a successful career, what's the secret?" He replied matter-of-factly, "centerfield." What? Centerfield? Anyone who knows me knows I'm a baseball fanatic. But, even as an avid baseball fan I had no idea what centerfield had to do with getting ahead or with having a successful career. So, as much as I wanted not to ask, I had to ask. "What on Earth does centerfield have to do with the question I asked?"

He said, "Kevin, John Fogerty, the lead singer of my favorite music group (Creedence Clearwater Revival or CCR), just released a solo album[3]. On the album, there's a chart-

56

topping song of the same name. Here's a cassette tape (yikes, this was a long time ago). I want you to listen to the song and pay close attention to a phrase often repeated in the song. That phrase is your answer."

Well, I only had to listen to the song two or three times before I clued in to the answer. The phrase was "put me in coach." Now, I'll tell you I figured out the phrase but I still didn't have a clue what "put me in coach" had to do with getting ahead or having a successful career.

"Kevin", he said, "this isn't rocket science." "When the Air Force comes calling on you to do your part, to take the TDY no one else wants to take, to PCS[4] to your last choice on your dream sheet rather than your first choice, if your answer is "put me in coach" then you'll be on your way to a successful career."

---

[3] After a nine year absence from the music scene, John Fogerty released the album _Centerfield_ in 1985

[4] Permanent change of station is an assignment change requiring a move to a new location normally for anywhere between one and four years, depending on location and duty

Best When On

As an Airman stationed at RAF Chicksands in the late '80s, I was assigned to the 6950th Electronic Security Group's Dawg Flight, working the infamous 12 and 3 schedule (4 days 0700-1500, 4 swings 1500-2300, and 4 mids 2300-0700, followed by three days off). At about 0400 on the third mid shift (our eleventh consecutive duty day), I was talking to a co-worker about a doubleheader I planned to play with my baseball team outside of London after work that day.

In the middle of this conversation, my supervisor walked over and sat down. My supervisor had that sixth sense I thought was reserved only for Mothers. You know, the ability to know what you're thinking, planning, or doing before you even think, plan, or do it. After listening for a moment he chimed in with, "Slater, read the label, it says *'Best When On'*."

As I had so many times before when getting advice or direction from my supervisor, I wondered what on Earth he was talking about. Within seconds, he said, "Haven't you seen a food label? It usually reads 'best by' followed by a date. Well, your brain has a label too. It reads, *'Best When On'*."

He continued, "now that I've got your attention, let me know if I understand your current plan correctly. You think it's a good idea to wake at 2100 last night in preparation for a 2300 mission show time; work an 8-hr shift (2300-0700); drive home, change clothes, grab your baseball equipment, and jump back into your car at 0900 for a three hour drive; start play at 1300; finish play at 1830; drive three hours home; shower, change, and report for work again tonight at 2300 for another 8-hr mid shift? Now if I do my math correctly, you plan to show up for the last of our mid shifts tonight after having been awake for over 24 hours? And worse than this, you plan to drive three hours from the baseball field to the base after having been awake for 22 ½ hours? Can you say 'dumber than dirt'? Now turn your brain on (it works much better that way) and rethink your plan."

My supervisor and I spent the next 20 minutes developing a plan which would keep me off the road (I left my car home and rode with a well-rested teammate), allow me to play ball, and return me to duty mission-ready.

I learned two important lessons that day. One, Air Force leadership isn't trying to prevent me from enjoying life. In fact, they're interested in helping me have a longer life to enjoy. So, *before* I bungee jump off a platform, I double-check my knot. *Before* I jump on my motorcycle, I double-check my bike and my personal protective equipment and wear all of it, on *and* off base. And *before* I go out to enjoy an 'adult beverage' I make a plan (and that plan **never** includes me driving myself home). And lesson number two? My supervisor was right. My brain definitely works 'best when on'. I've made it a habit ever since to make sure the first thing I do each morning is make sure my on/off switch is in the right position.

Bumper Cars

I have fond memories as a young boy spending a lot of my time and my parents' money on one of my favorite carnival rides, bumper cars. The whole point of the ride was to crash into other riders as violently as possible, while evading their attempts to crash into you.

Unlike the lawless world of bumper cars, there are many rules we're required to follow when operating a motor vehicle on our base and in our community. It may seem like these rules are in place to cramp our driving style, but they're really here to ensure the personal safety of every member of our team. I wonder if some of my teammates also grew up as fans of bumper cars. Unfortunately, it seems too many of us drive our cars and trucks the same way we drove our bumper cars—with reckless disregard for ourselves and others. Have you ever read an installation security forces blotter[5]? On an almost daily basis there are some scary driving practices littering the blotter.

How does someone back out of a parking space and into another car, a wall, a pole, or other fixed, inanimate object? It's unlikely the other car, the wall, or the pole leapt into the car's path. My guess is the culprit is haste. Why else would we not bother to do a 'walk around' of our vehicle to ensure there are no objects in our path before backing up or

---

[5] An accounting of all activity occurring in a 24-hour period requiring accountability or response by security forces

pulling out? Why else wouldn't our passenger act as a spotter when we're backing up and then jump into our vehicle only after all obstacles have been avoided? Why are we willing to risk so much (damage, injury, or death) for so little (a few moments of time)?

Often the only damage is to cars, concrete, and poles, and the only injury to egos. But what happens when the inevitable occurs and we start hitting our teammates?

I worry every time I see someone operating their vehicle on base while texting or talking on a hand-held cell phone[6]. I will often follow Mr. or Ms. Chatty to their final destination to remind them (in the nicest possible way of course) of our traffic safety rules and their purpose. In every case, I find a courteous person behind the wheel—our teammates are not disregarding our rules because they're bad people—I believe they disregard our rules simply out of ignorance of the potential consequences of their behavior. I hope they never find themselves having to explain how being on the phone while driving had nothing to do with running over one of us in a crosswalk or in a parking lot.

To avoid harming one of my teammates, I promise to put my bumper cars game face on only at carnivals, to put my phone away before starting my car, to invest a few extra seconds for a safety walk around my vehicle before backing

---

[6] Neither of these activities is permitted on any Department of Defense installation

out of my parking spot, and to be a spotter for the driver when I'm a passenger in a vehicle. On behalf of your teammates, would you mind if I asked you to make the same promise? While bumper cars are fun, driving on base and in our community is definitely not a carnival ride.

MSF Training Rules!

In the immortal words of Steppenwolf's *Born to be Wild*, "get your motor running ... head out on the highway ... looking for adventure ... whatever comes our way ..."[7] In the few years I've been a motorcycle rider--yes I'm a late bloomer, it took me twenty years to wear down my wife before she finally gave me the ok--the words to this song echo in my head every time I strap on my helmet. Although this great 'wind therapy' anthem has my head rockin' as I tighten my chin strap, there are also other words kicking around inside my head--the words of my Motorcycle Safety Foundation (MSF)[8] course instructor. He constantly reminded all the participants in our class, "time and distance are your friends. Take your time and keep your distance." Thankfully this quote is one I've never forgotten. In fact, this quote may very well have saved my skin.

It was back a few years ago on a dusty patch of Loop 1604 in San Antonio, Texas. With a great deal of encouragement from Steppenwolf, I was motoring south on 1604 at a point where it's only a single lane in each direction. I was trailing a pickup truck straight off the set of Sanford & Son.[9] You know, the rusted bucket of bolts full of kitchen appliances, copper pipe, and yard trash. As soon as I spotted

---

[7] *Born to be Wild* released in 1968 — the band's most successful single off their debut album
[8] International developer of rider education and training
[9] Sanford and Son - an American TV sitcom (1972 to 1977)

the truck, the words of my MSF instructor began echoing in my head "... keep your distance." I backed off the throttle, sacrificing speed for distance--giving myself more time to react should something fly loose from the bungee-corded mess barely strapped inside the bed of this wreckage on wheels.

Thankfully, that afternoon the words of my MSF instructor won out over the words of Steppenwolf. No sooner had I backed off the throttle, what appeared to be the twisted carcass of an old washing machine came bounding off the tailgate of the truck striking the road in front of me. Distance was my friend that day, as I was able to avoid the debris by steering around the shrapnel strewn across the highway.

Air Force leadership may have saved my skin that day too. I wonder, would I have taken the MSF Basic Rider course if it wasn't mandated for all Airmen? Would I have heard the words "time and distance are your friends"? Would Steppenwolf's words have been the only ones on my mind when I rolled up behind that bucket of bolts? Would I have been too close to respond safely when the washing machine fell off the truck? These questions will go unanswered.

While I can't be sure what may have happened on Loop 1604 that day if I'd not attended MSF training, I am sure of one thing. I sure am glad my leadership was looking out for me when they mandated MSF Basic Rider training. Steppenwolf rocks, but motorcycle riding with MSF training rules!

Good Pain

Have you ever seen the words 'good' and 'pain' side-by-side in the same sentence before? I clearly remember when I was first introduced to this phrase.

Air Force Instruction 36-2618 *'The Little Brown Book'*, paragraph 4.1.14., directs NCOs to provide career counseling to subordinates. Well, long before the birth of the *Little Brown Book*, my supervisor conducted annual career counseling sessions with every one of his Airmen. It was during one of those sessions I was introduced to the notion of 'good pain'.

My supervisor was explaining Air Force benefits, entitlements, and opportunities available to me when he paused and said, "Kevin, here's the bottom line. Whether you'll be an ordinary or extraordinary Airman will likely depend on your willingness to experience 'good pain'." Good pain? I wasn't sure what he meant by this oxymoron, but I'd learned from previous conversations with my supervisor to give him a minute or two; he'd eventually provide a translation I could understand.

He said, "Kevin, are you willing to do what you *need* to do and not just what you *want* to do? More importantly, will you do those things so many others are unwilling to do? Let me give you a few examples of what I'm talking about."

When you have the option to roll over for an extra hour of sleep or to crawl out of bed to hit the road for PT[10],

---

[10] PT – physical training or physical fitness activities

which will you choose? Will sleep win every morning until you're a week away from your PT test? As the world's most well-rested couch potato, will you then expect to cram a year's worth of fitness into a week's activity and then blame failure on everything but yourself?

When you're one class shy of your Community College of the Air Force (CCAF) degree and that last class happens to be your least favorite subject, will you enroll, suck it up, and get 'er done or will you wake up one day as a Master Sergeant (MSgt) unable to get promoted to Senior Master Sergeant (SMSgt) or to serve as the best example for your Airmen and NCOs because you put off one class, one measly three-credit class, one your peers did ten or more years ago? Will you then spend more time badmouthing the value of CCAF or the unfair expectation levied on you than it would have taken you to complete the class in the first place?

When you're invited to enroll in the Senior Noncommissioned Officer (SNCO) Academy correspondence course the day after you get your line number for MSgt[11], will you enroll, bust your butt, and knock it out or will you engage your supervisor in a buffoonerous discussion of the dictionary definition of the word 'should' because you're 'smart enough' to know *The Little Brown Book* doesn't say 'must' or

---

[11] A Technical Sergeant with two years time-in-grade and who has already graduated from the NCO Academy may also enroll in the SNCO Academy correspondence course

'mandatory'? I know what your supervisor 'should' do at the end of that conversation; I think you do too, don't you?

I'm glad my supervisor introduced me to the concept of 'good pain' that day. If he hadn't, I may not have learned how to appropriately respond when my leadership's expectations of me didn't line up perfectly with my own. I may have made too many choices in favor of my own wishes over those of the Air Force, my unit, and the Airmen I was responsible for. How disastrous that may have been for the Air Force, my unit, and the Airmen who saw me as 'the example' to follow.

I'm no glutton for punishment, but I'm definitely a believer in the value of 'good pain', especially if it involves something which will make me a better Wingman, Leader, or Warrior.

I'm Impressed!

In the thirteen months I served as a member of the 1st Fighter Wing I watched a Senior Airman in our wing interact professionally with all whom she came into contact. I watched this same Senior Airman give her best every duty day. I also watched her make her way through a dog-eared copy of the Professional Development Guide[12] during her lunch break and after duty hours. I watched her carry a backpack full of college textbooks on her back at the end of a duty day headed for night school. But just when I thought I'd seen her do it all, she did a few more things that just impressed the heck out of me.

One afternoon, our wing protocol officer asked this Senior Airman if she'd be willing to perform proffer[13] duty during our upcoming change-of-command. What was her immediate response? Yes, of course. Now you might think, what's the big deal about proffer duty? Performing proffer duty impresses you Chief? Well, no, not exactly. Here's what does impress me. This Senior Airman had just packed her personal belongings (including service dress coat) and placed them in long-term storage as she prepared to leave for a 179-day deployment to the United States Central Command

---

[12] The Professional Development Guide or PDG is a desktop resource intended for the professional growth of our Airmen (it also serves as the guide upon which enlisted promotion examinations are based)

[13] The proffer accounts for, aligns, and handles all material required for presentation at a ceremony

(USCENTCOM) AOR. Did she say she couldn't do proffer duty because she'd packed her service coat? No. Instead of responding with "I'd love to, but I can't", she contacted a wingman who shared her coat size and borrowed her service coat. And, oh yeah, she purchased a new service coat nametag too (she had packed hers with her service coat of course).

Bottom line: Where was this Airman during the change-of-command? On stage of course, doing everything a proffer is required to do. And, that's not all.

This Senior Airman recently dropped her daughter off with grandma and grandpa. Yes, she'll be on the rotator[14] any day now headed for the AOR, missing her toddler dearly. She has been nothing short of remarkable in stepping up to her duty—I haven't heard one negative word escape this Senior Airman's lips from the moment she was tasked to fulfill this deployment (even though we can be sure her daughter will do and experience many 'firsts' while Mom is away—those things a Mom will hate to miss).

This Senior Airman's deployment departure was then delayed a few days due to shuffling rotator schedules. A stroke of good luck as it turns out. She had recently completed the final class required for a Community College of the Air Force[15] degree in her career field. But, that's not what impressed me.

---

[14] Aircraft delivering military personnel to/from the Area of Responsibility (AOR) or combat zone

[15] The Community College of the Air Force (CCAF) is the world's largest community college; has awarded over 300,000 associate in applied science degrees

What impressed me was she made a second call to her wingman to borrow that same service coat, once again forsaking the opportunity to utter "I'd love to, but I can't".

Bottom line: Where was this Airman during the commencement ceremony last week? She was right where she belonged—crossing the stage to receive her diploma. That's not all. She was one of only 10 of our 180 graduates on base to earn an Air Force Association (AFA)-sponsored Pitsenbarger Award[16].

Last Thursday, as I sat in Fort Myer's Memorial Chapel, one of many Airmen paying final respects to our 1st Chief Master Sergeant of the Air Force, CMSAF Paul Airey, as he was laid to rest, I reflected on his words inscribed on the north wall of the Air Force Memorial in Washington D.C., "When I think of the enlisted force, I see dedication, determination, loyalty and valor." I thought of him, his words, and Senior Airman (SrA) Nicole Harley. I think he'd be glad to know Senior Airman Nicole Harley is doing everything she can to live up to his words. I think he'd be impressed. I know I am.

---

[16] Pitsenbarger Awards provide a one-time grant of $400 to selected active duty, Guard and Reserve enlisted graduates of CCAF who plan to pursue a baccalaureate degree

Right 10, Left 32, Right 18

One evening on the night shift as a young NCO, I approached my supervisor looking for some advice on how to better communicate with my subordinates. I was having an incredibly difficult time connecting with or getting through to my Airmen. I had no clue why each one responded differently to my attempts to engage with them. I was hoping for answers, an explanation, or at least some sound advice. Instead what I got was another one of those cryptic responses my supervisor was famous for delivering to me. He said "right 10, left 32, right 18." And I said "what?" I was struggling to connect with my Airmen and he was quoting the combination to the lock on our storage closet.

"Kevin", he said, "every one of your Airmen is an individual. Each has differences in personality, hopes, aspirations, and dreams. Each one values things differently. Your Airmen may all look the same, much like combination locks look the same when hanging on a shelf in the hardware store, yet each Airman will respond differently to different motivators, much like a lock responds only to its own combination. Dialing right 10, left 32, right 18 on every lock in this building will only open this one lock (the one on our unit's storage closet). If you try to dial in to every Airman in exactly the same way, you may get through to one of them, but you almost certainly won't get through to all of them."

71

"Why would you expect to get the same response from every one of your Airmen using the same approach? People are as different as combination locks. What one person values highly another loathes, what one aspires to, another is indifferent to. If you're going to get the most from each of your Airmen, you're going to have to learn what makes them tick and then exercise situational leadership. You're going to have to figure out the combination which works for each of your Airmen."

And now for the epiphany: He said, "It's not your Airman's responsibility to open up to you when he doesn't recognize the 'combination' you're dialing. It's up to you to discover which 'combination' motivates your Airman. If you truly want to get the most from your Airmen, you're going to have to invest in learning as much as you can about them. What do they value? Why are they here? Most importantly though, how are you going to tie their goals to unit and Air Force goals? How are you going to find out their combination? Are you going to try to crack them like a safe (using a stethoscope and some C4 (explosives) is not a likely path to success) or will you adapt your communication methods well enough to cause them to willingly disclose their combination to you?"

Being Mr. Underwood

Mr. Joseph Underwood[17] would make a great Air Force leader. As I traveled to Montgomery, Alabama recently to support our professional military education graduates, I picked up a newspaper to read aboard my flight. I came across an article outlining Mr. Underwood's background, teaching methods, successes, and subsequent nomination for a national-level teaching award. Several things in the article stood out as lessons in leadership more so than simply the attributes of a good teacher.

One of Mr. Underwood's High School students now interning as an on-camera newscaster for a local media company paid tribute to Mr. Underwood by saying, "in my sophomore year he pulled me aside and told me he saw something in me….he saw that I could do this. He gave me my future. He gave me an opportunity, and I took it."

Just as Mr. Underwood had done for this student, I see our best leaders diligently assessing our personnel to discover untapped talent—their passionate interest inspiring each of them to perform. Mr. Underwood revealed his leadership secret later in the article (funny how the best methods often appear so simple), "Every time I tried to do something in my life, there was someone behind me who said "You can do this. You will do this. I will get you what you

---

[17] Miami High School TV Production and Filmmaking teacher

73

need to succeed. I want to be that person for my students." I saw three powerful things in Mr. Underwood's comments:

1) When he tried something, he had supporters proclaiming "you CAN and WILL do this."

2) His supporters were active. "I will get you what you need to succeed" NOT "I hope you make it." His supporters willingly shared responsibility for his success/failure.

3) Mr. Underwood understood his supporters' expectations for payback in the form of transitioning from supported to supporter when the right moment presented itself. He actually looked forward to assuming the role of supporter for someone else in need of an inspirational believer (a mentor).

Every promotion in grade or position (officer, enlisted, or civilian) also serves as a signal to transition further from supported to supporter. I'm thankful supervisors throughout my career understood when it was time for them to 'be Mr. Underwood'. I look forward to teaming with you to build Airmen (officer, enlisted, and civilian) who realize their full potential—I look forward to 'being Mr. Underwood'.

When is a Wall Not a Wall?

Earlier in the book, in _Professional Courtesy_, I told the story of my excitement when applying for a position in the U.S. Embassy in Moscow, Russia. I've had a number of Airmen approach me to ask, "Hey Chief, whatever happened? Did you get the assignment?"

No, I never did get the assignment. And, so here's the rest of the story.

On Monday morning, I called the number in the ad and had to complete an oral interview in Russian. I thought I did well—and I had the impression my interviewer thought the same. However, once we began to complete the required documents everything came to a screeching halt. "Name?" asked the interviewer. "Kevin George Slater" I replied. "Grade?" inquired the interviewer. "Senior Airman" I responded. "Senior Airman? Oh, I'm sorry but you must be an NCO to be selected for Embassy duty," said the interviewer. I was stunned.

I'll save you from the long, drawn out version of the rest of the story but I never did get the assignment. I wasn't an NCO. To say I was disappointed would be to put it mildly. I was fuming. I simply couldn't understand why they'd turn down a fully qualified candidate simply because I wasn't an NCO. What difference did that make?

When I got to work that night, I told my supervisor the whole story. Oh yeah, he got the full length version—he was very patient. When I got to the end of my story I fully expected him to tell me how he was going to help me, how he was going to call someone, how I shouldn't worry, how he was going to fix everything. Of course, that's not what happened at all.

He looked me straight in the eye and said, "Airman Slater, when is a wall not a wall?"

By now you clearly understand my supervisor had a knack for confusing me with crazy responses to my questions or dilemmas. I'd normally walk away shaking my head, wondering what the heck he was talking about. But I couldn't this time. He had my attention. When is a wall not a wall? Huh?

He said, "Airman Slater, sometimes a wall isn't a wall, it's a test. It may not be as simple as you cannot have this assignment. It may be how *badly* do you want this assignment? Are you willing to wait? Are you willing to study, get promoted, and then re-apply? Maybe this is the motivation you need to study for Staff Sergeant this cycle. Is this defeat or a temporary stop on your way to your desired destination?" Wow! He was right ... even if I still didn't understand some of the crazy stuff he often said.

So, when is a wall not a wall? That's easy. When the wall is not an obstacle preventing you from an opportunity, but is simply a test of how hard you're willing to work to get that opportunity.

76

Promotion Test 'No-Show'

Several NCOs have been 'no-shows' for enlisted promotion testing this test cycle. Like the rest of us, they're human. One simply remembered his test date incorrectly and didn't realize it until after his actual test date had passed. Another showed up at the wrong place, another at the wrong time. You might think, "What's the big deal? We'll just make new appointments." Well, you'd be wrong to think it's as simple as that. The rules are quite strict for a variety of reasons. The increased potential for test compromise, the perception of unfairly gaining additional study time, and the impact of extending the test cycle if there are many requests are just a few of the reasons.

No one likes the 'taste' of a 'no second chances' policy. But, I have to tell you in almost all cases members will not get a second chance. Failing to report for scheduled testing renders an Airman ineligible for promotion consideration unless the commander (typically the installation's Force Support Squadron (FSS) Commander) approves rescheduling. Reasons such as oversleeping, marking the wrong date or time on the calendar, reporting to the wrong building or room, forgetting the test date, failing to show in military uniform, failing to bring military identification card, or simply being late are not normally considered valid reasons and rescheduling typically won't be authorized.

What can you do to avoid this dilemma when it's your turn to test? When you sign for your test date, carefully note your test date, time, and location. Mark it on a calendar at home and on a calendar in your duty section. Tell someone else the date. Double-check your alarm clock. Double-check your wallet or purse to ensure you have your ID card. Leave home well in advance of the time needed to arrive at the test location on time. Cover everything within your control.

Ultimately, these individuals are personally responsible for their actions and the resulting penalties. However, there is something to be said for teamwork. Members of the best teams know when each other is testing. They don't hand-hold. They are wingmen[18]—there's a difference. While they're not engaged in every aspect of each other's lives, they are engaged in those events with the most significant impact on each others' professional lives.

The harsh penalties applied should laser focus our attention on ensuring we're engaged, preferably before problems arise. When that's not possible, we do the next best thing and alert others to the issue before it affects them too. This story won't help these NCOs, but maybe it will help to prevent the next unnecessary 'no show'. Please pass the word—be a good Wingman.

---

[18] Wingman – The Air Force's Wingman Concept is based on the idea that we're to look after each other. Just as the wingman in a flight formation has responsibilities to the flight lead, so does every Airman to one another

Reenlistment Bonuses: Good for All

Some time ago, I shared an updated list of selective reenlistment bonuses with a group of people. I'll admit I was surprised by the number of people who misunderstood the value of reenlistment bonuses, believing it was good news ONLY for those people fortunate enough to be in career fields receiving bonuses. I believe bonuses are great news EVEN if your career field is NOT on the list. A shortsighted view of the value of bonuses could potentially come back to bite someone later on. Please follow me through this scenario:

Let's say you're a 3D0X1 (Knowledge Operations Management) and you love your job. You've been in the field for 10 years and wouldn't want to do anything else. Your field isn't on the Selective Reenlistment Bonus (SRB) list. So, you decide the list is unimportant to you—in fact, you ignore it. Maybe you even believe bonuses are unfair (someone is getting extra cash and you're not—that can't be fair).

One day, the Air Force decides "let's no longer offer bonuses for critical shortage career fields because we might hurt the feelings of people whose career fields are not on the list."

So, lots of people in critical shortage fields suddenly decide to get out because the Air Force has cut off the compensation (bonuses) they had been receiving as . an incentive to continue to face the increased risks of their field (Explosive Ordnance Disposal (EOD), Pararescue (PJ), etc), to

79

overlook higher salaries in the civilian/contractor world (computer operations/maintenance), or to cover the high cost of lengthy Air Force training (Linguist).

As a result of this greater exodus of fully trained Airmen, the Air Force says "Hmmm, we now need to retrain some folks (possibly 3D0X1 for example) into an ever-increasing list of critical shortage career fields. In fact, we're going to have to forcibly retrain some folks because we'll never get enough volunteers to enter some of these fields (see reasons above) now that we don't offer any more incentives (bonuses)."

Suddenly the repercussions of not having bonuses could ultimately impact you. You're no longer a 3D0X1 (the job you love) and you're an EOD technician not receiving a bonus. Hmmm … this isn't sounding too good. So, in short, although we'd all love to have cash in the form of a selective reenlistment bonus, I'd say it would be shortsighted to suggest the only people who should care about bonuses are those folks who are currently receiving them.

One final note: Selective reenlistment bonuses are NOT in any way a values statement on the importance of the contributions or efforts of the members of a particular career field or series of career fields. Bottom line: SRBs are a retention tool, pure and simple, they are not an indicator of any career field(s) being any more valuable than any other(s).

Legacy

I recently attended three very special military events. First, I took leave to travel to San Antonio to attend the retirement of a special friend and mentor. Then, I attended Team Langley's Chiefs' Recognition Ceremony at our Bayside Enlisted Club. And finally, I witnessed the commissioning of the USS Bush at Naval Station Norfolk's Pier 14. Although each of these events were quite different, they shared a common theme – legacy.

Mr. Larry Oakes retired after 40 years of service as an Airman—4 years in uniform and 36 years as a Department of the Air Force civilian. Mr. Oakes is a special human being who, while always focused on the mission, never took his eye off of what was best for his people. What I'll remember most from his ceremony is a comment he made at the end of his remarks. Just when I expected him to say he was ready to go fishing or to go golfing, he instead said he's looking forward to using his time in retirement to pay back his life's good fortune. Even in retirement Mr. Oakes is thinking of someone other than himself.

At our Chiefs' Recognition Ceremony, I listened as Chief Master Sergeant of the Air Force #12 (ret) Eric Benken talked to us about pride in our uniform, our mission, and the people with whom we work. He put special emphasis on "the people" as he relayed a story from his time as an Airman. If not for a life-changing conversation with Chief Master

Sergeant (CMSgt) Lee, who helped Airman Benken realize what the Air Force really had to offer him, we may very well have had a different 12th Chief Master Sergeant of the Air Force.

Finally, I witnessed the Commissioning of the USS George H.W. Bush. I could hear humbled tones in former President George H.W. Bush's voice as he remarked on the commissioning of his namesake, the world's most advanced aircraft carrier and the last of its kind--a fitting tribute to an honorable Naval Aviator, officer, and former President.

The legacy of these three men; Mr. Larry Oakes, CMSgt Lee, and former President George H.W. Bush can be summed up by a quote from Jackie Robinson[19], a man you may know as a Brooklyn Dodger, but whose life was much bigger than baseball itself. Jackie Robinson once said, "A life is not important except in the impact it has on other lives."

Within each of us is the ability to impact the life of another--maybe on a moment's notice—maybe without any notice. Will you recognize the opportunity when it presents itself? What will be your legacy?

---

[19] Jack Roosevelt "Jackie" Robinson (31 Jan 1919 – 24 Oct 1972) was the first black major league baseball player of the modern era. Robinson broke the baseball color barrier when he debuted with the Brooklyn Dodgers in 1947

The Birth of our Nation

On the eve of the first day of fighting on the now hallowed grounds of Gettysburg, Pennsylvania, Colonel Joshua Chamberlain, Commander of the 20th Maine was delivered a most challenging conundrum: How do you *force* men to fight for freedom? One hundred twenty war-weary men of the 2nd Maine Regiment, having lost half their brothers to the eleven battles the regiment had participated in since marching out of Bangor, Maine, more than two years earlier, had been forced-marched as mutineers to Colonel Chamberlain's location for refusing to engage in further battles. It was now Colonel Chamberlain's duty to convince them to rejoin the fight, to shoot them for refusing to do their duty, or to escort them under guard to eventual courts-martial.

There isn't enough space in this short story for me to recount everything Colonel Chamberlain shared with the men of the 2nd Maine Regiment that day on the road to Gettysburg nearly 150 years ago, so I'll focus on two themes that have stuck with me since I first read them many years ago in _The Killer Angels_, by Michael Shaara[20].

First, he spoke to the moral virtues of that day's Army. "This is a different kind of Army. If you look at history you'll see men fight for pay, or women, or some other kind of loot.

---

[20] Michael Shaara, 1928-1988, served as a Sergeant in the 82d Airborne Division prior to the Korean War; awarded the Pulitzer Prize for _The Killer Angels_ in 1975

They fight for land, or a king, or because they like killing. But we're here for something new. We're an Army out to set other men free."

Second, he described perfectly what it meant to be an American and an American soldier. "This is free ground all the way from here to the Pacific Ocean. No man bows. No man is born to royalty. Here you're judged on what you do, not by what your father was. Here you can be something. Here's a place to build a home. It isn't the land, there's always more land. It's the idea that we all have value ... you and I ... we're worth something more than the dirt. I never saw dirt I'd die for, but I'm not asking you to come join us and fight for dirt. What we're all fighting for, in the end, is each other."

All but six of the one hundred twenty men of the 2nd Maine voluntarily took up arms and joined their 20th Maine brothers that day to continue to fight for the uniquely American values and virtues so eloquently described by Col Joshua Chamberlain.

As you light your barbecues, fellowship with family and friends, enjoy a trip to the outlet mall, or simply sneak away for a relaxing moment with your feet up each Fourth of July, please reflect on the words of Joshua Chamberlain as you decide what it is you're celebrating. Is it the Declaration of Independence, the Revolutionary War, the drafting of the Constitution, or is it the idea of self-determination declared within, fought for, and codified by these very things? I'm mindful of the many things I have to be thankful for, including a life of opportunity based on merit rather than by birthright. Thanks for all you've done and will continue to do to ensure this very American idea continues to thrive.

<u>Our Flag: Long May She Wave</u>

On 14 June, 1777 the Continental Congress passed the first 'Flag Act' establishing a flag for our new nation. For over 230 years, our flag has served in times of trouble and triumph as a universal symbol of the strength, courage, and commitment of the American spirit. When I see it wave, I am humbled.

I see the Minutemen at Concord and hear Lincoln's Gettysburg Address.

I understand Robert E. Lee's courageous surrender at Appomattox courthouse and remain in awe of American resolve in WWI and WWII.

I see our colors flying proudly over Ebbett's Field as Jackie Robinson trots out to 1st base.

I witness Neil Armstrong and Buzz Aldrin planting our flag on the surface of the moon.

I see the flag-draped coffin of JFK as the caisson carries him to Arlington National cemetery. But, more importantly, I am amazed by our republic's smooth transition of presidential powers.

Old School is Good School

I hear Ronald Reagan implore Mr. Gorbachev to "tear down this wall" and I have the opportunity to be assigned to Berlin as an NCO and watch it happen with my own eyes.

I see today's basic trainees earn the privilege to be called Airmen and I see them march proudly at graduation across the parade field at Lackland Air Force Base, the Gateway to the Air Force.

I see the men and women, the officers, enlisted, and civilians, active, guard, and reserve, of the best installations across our United States Air Force. I see in each member the same strength, courage, and commitment of the American spirit symbolized by our great flag.

On the anniversary of this act (now known as Flag Day), I invite you to spend a moment reflecting on what our flag means to you. Our flag, long may she wave!

A Proud Heritage

On 18 April 1942, 52 officers and 28 enlisted men volunteered to lead a historic joint expeditionary tasking—The Doolittle Raid. These 80 Airmen conducted America's first assault on Japan in retaliation for the attack on Pearl Harbor. The mission required Airmen and Sailors to launch bombers (B-25) into combat for the first time off the deck of an aircraft carrier (USS Hornet).

At a desperate time in our nation's history, 80 warriors answered their nation's call to fly, fight, and win. These volunteers launched 16 B-25s off a rolling carrier deck more than 600 miles from Tokyo. Flying on fumes (no air-to-air refueling at that time) and damaged by anti-aircraft fire, our bombers limped toward the Chinese coast after releasing their ordnance over Japan. Our Airmen landed in hostile Russia, ditched in the sea, or bailed out over China.

A few died before reaching China, eight were captured and held as POWs by the Japanese (three of them executed), and many risked capture by helping the injured to move slowly through Chinese territory occupied by Japanese soldiers. The 80 Distinguished Flying Crosses, two Silver Stars, and one Medal of Honor earned by these heroes add immensely to our proud heritage, tradition of honor, and legacy of valor.

I am humbled to know our proud heritage extends from men like Lt Gen Jimmy Doolittle, Maj Ted Lawson, SGT David Thatcher, and CPL Bert Jordan all the way to me (and to those who will follow me). Do their actions add to my sense of purpose? You bet! Am I proud of my service's history? You bet--and you should be too. Each one of you contributes to our legacy, be you an Airman Basic, a Chief, a Lieutenant, or General.

We stand as 21st Century guardians of freedom and justice; our nation's sword and shield; its sentry and avenger. Whether engaged in active combat operations or in support of operations to avenge the loss of American lives at the hands of terrorists, we should be proud of our actions as wingmen, leaders, and warriors pledged to never leave another behind; committed to never falter; endeavoring to never fail.

If you'd like to learn more about the Doolittle Raid, I recommend *The First Heroes*, authored by Craig Nelson.[21]

---

[21] Craig Nelson is the author of *Rocket Men*, *The First Heroes*, *Thomas Paine* (winner of the 2007 Henry Adams Prize), and *Let's Get Lost* (short-listed for W.H. Smith's Book of the Year)

Avoid 'Coulda, Shoulda, Woulda'

My wife Linda and I recently rolled our motorcycles into the driveway at the end of a 1,500 mile roundtrip ride to New Mexico for a fellow Chief's retirement ceremony. We started planning this 'wind therapy' road trip a few months in advance. In many ways, this trip reminded me of our almost-2,000 mile 25th wedding anniversary ride to Niagara Falls a few years ago. Yes, we've been married a long time. Although I'll tell you, it seems like only yesterday. When many young newlyweds find out how long we've been married, one of their first questions is, "how'd you do it?" It's pretty hard to answer that question with a short response, but I believe the best short answer is, we've avoided 'coulda, shoulda, woulda'.

Why is this important? I'm convinced our lives have flourished because we've always supported each other's need to set and achieve goals, individually and as a couple.

We decided to join the Air Force in 1984 and have never looked back. Whether we moved far from family and friends, served overseas, faced family separation due to Temporary Duty (TDY), deployment, or Permanent Change of Station (PCS), we chose to view it as opportunity rather than hardship and to support each other's effort to grow from the experience, and I'm glad we did. We've literally been living the old saying, "time flies when you're having fun" ever since.

During our many years together, we've lived everywhere, made life-long friends from foreign lands, and raised two boys who saw moves from school to school as opportunities and not as ready-made excuses for poor performance or social hardship. When our eldest son planned to move far from home to attend college, we weren't selfish enough to talk him out of it. We'd love to have had him close by, but couldn't have him saying 'coulda, shoulda, woulda' years later.

When I was invited to serve as the Command Chief for a Wing in Southwest Asia, Linda immediately supported my decision to leap at the offer. She knew how much I valued the opportunity to serve our Airmen in combat. Just before my departure, Linda decided she was going to learn how to ride a motorcycle (I'd been riding for five years by then), so we'd have the opportunity to share 'wind therapy' moments when I returned from a year in the desert. Rather than talk her out of it, I did my best to support her by spending many hours in our cul-de-sac teaching her to look, press, lean, and roll. 6,000+ miles on two wheels later, she's doing great.

What's the secret to marital bliss? I have no idea. I doubt anyone does. But, what's the secret to a fun life worth sharing with someone else? Support each others' wish to live, learn, and grow—don't ever be the reason your partner is found saying 'coulda, shoulda, woulda'. Fitting in a 1,500 mile 'wind therapy' session at least once a year is not a bad idea either.

I approach every task focused on superior
accomplishment and performance.

<u>Chapter 3</u>

<u>EXCELLENCE IN ALL WE DO</u>

I actively seek opportunities for myself and my
Airmen to achieve comprehensive fitness;
physical, mental, social, and spiritual.

Belief: A High Performance Fuel

Setting the bar high may establish a climate of high expectations but it won't necessarily result in high performance. At the end of the day whether you think you can or think you can't—you're right[1]. Belief is the difference maker. A high bar simply brings high expectations (High Bar = High Expectations). Add belief to your high bar and you'll get high performance (High Bar + Belief = High Performance). Why is this important to note? Well, high performance will deliver mission accomplishment (High Performance = Mission Accomplishment).

If you think you're beaten, you are;

If you think that you dare not, you don't;

If you'd like to win, but think you can't,

It's almost certain you won't.

If you think you'll lose, you've lost;

For out in the world you'll find

Success begins with a fellows will.

It's all in the state of mind.

---

[1] Quote attributed to Henry Ford (1863-1947), American industrialist and pioneer of the assembly-line production method

Old School is Good School

If you think you are outclassed, you are;
You've got to think high to rise;
You've got to be sure of yourself before
You can ever win a prize.

Life's battles don't always go
To the stronger or faster man;
But sooner or later the man who wins
Is the man who thinks he can.

Author Unknown

For decades, distance runners attempted to break the four-minute mile while dozens of medical journals proclaimed it physically impossible. Doctor's opinions were simply accepted as fact. Then, in 1954 Roger Bannister accomplished the impossible by running a mile in 3:59.4. Within three years, 16 other runners also broke the four-minute barrier. Did human beings suddenly become faster? Or was 'the bar' finally hurdled by ability fueled by belief?

Don't set limits on what you believe is possible. Self-imposed limitations may be the only thing between you and a promotion, a college degree, or achieving your childhood dreams. Don't be a naysayer, be a doer. Turning the impossible into the possible is often not a factor of ability but a factor of belief. I'm proud to be a member of the Air Force, a high performance organization … where we fuel high expectations with belief every day!

My Mess Dress Got Promoted Today

A few years ago, in an effort to generate enthusiasm on the part of my wing's Airmen to participate in an upcoming Enlisted Dining In[2], I made the following offer. "If you audition for Madame or Mister Vice[3] and you're selected to fill the role, and you don't already own a Mess Dress[4], I will buy you one." I'm no marketing genius, but I do know people love FREE stuff.

Overnight, I went from one volunteer to twenty-one. In fact, Airmen from my wing were selected to serve as Madame AND Mister Vice. Mister Vice already owned a Mess Dress that needed some updating (new stripes and medals) which I gladly paid for. Madame Vice was a high-energy Airman First Class who I gladly walked with to military clothing sales that day to part with a few hundred of my hard-earned dollars.

I had no problem doing something unusual, something a little unorthodox, or maybe even something a little nutty if it was going to lead to greater participation on the part of my Airmen in an event full of military customs and traditions. My only hope was their participation would lead to a greater sense of belonging, the desire to get even more

---

[2] Formal military function designed to build Esprit de Corps
[3] Emcees and event choreographers at a Dining In/Out
[4] Formal wear for Air Force members at a Dining In/Out (not issued to enlisted personnel; costs approximately $400)

involved, and the chance they'd one day look back on that day as a difference-maker in their military career.

Well, not only did Madame Vice look great as the lowest ranking member of the Mess[5] in a Mess Dress, but she knocked the Madame Vice role out of the park (attitude definitely is everything). I was never left wondering whether I'd made a good decision. You can bet my Airmen knew I was dead serious about finding ways for them to get engaged, even if I had to put my money where my mouth was (this proved to be one of the best investments I ever made).

In my mind, my decision required no further validation. But, sometimes life is funny about delivering messages to you; often when you least expect them.

I received an invitation to attend a promotion pin-on ceremony for a young Staff Sergeant to-be. A1C Bridgett Kramer, no longer an A1C, had obviously rocketed right through Senior Airman on a VFR direct[6] course to NCO and had asked if I'd be able to attend. I wouldn't have missed it!

As SSgt Bridgett Kramer addressed the crowd in attendance I couldn't have been more proud. She thanked everyone from her husband to her supervisors to her peers (one of those moments where you know the Air Force promotes the right people). Wow! My Mess Dress got promoted today! I'm so proud.

---

[5] The Mess is the assembled personnel at a Dining In/Out
[6] Visual Flight Rules (VFR) – aviation term; pilot flies using landmarks instead of instruments; suggests direct route

You See It, You Own It

Throughout my career, I've found our best leaders to be those who've worked hardest to ingrain in our members a sense of belonging; a sense of community; a sense of ownership. Consequently, I've never understood the willingness on the part of some leaders to sign up our Airmen to do the dumbest of tasks. For example, take the typical, knee-jerk reaction to a commander sharing that he's "seen a lot of trash on the ground around here lately".

In the blink of an eye, I see teams of Airmen whose sole responsibility it will now be to walk the grounds of our building or the entire base searching for, collecting, and disposing of trash. Wow, if this isn't dumber than dirt!

Someone in a position of authority or influence comments on trash being in the yard (no specifics as to how much, where, and dropped by whom) and the next thing you know we're assigning details to walk the yard for several hours a day, every day, whether it needs it or not? Huh? Am I missing something? This doesn't appear very effective on so many levels:

1. Someone is organizing and accounting for the detail—which means they're not doing their real job

2. Someone is conducting the detail—which means they're also not doing their real job---and they're conducting the

detail 'cause the schedule says to do so (whether there's trash in the yard or not)—yikes!

3. Despite the detail there's no guarantee the yard will be free of trash (someone may toss trash in the yard after the detail is done for the day—then what? Does it sit there until the next day's detail?)

4. Not everyone is conducting the detail (generally done only by junior personnel or that segment of the population one can direct to do the detail), so not all are invested in the yard's condition

I say **STOP** the madness! Why don't we adopt a very simple philosophy of 'If you see it, you own it'? Under this philosophy, no one spends time organizing a detail, no one conducts the detail whether it needs to be done or not (everyone can go back to warfighting—what the American taxpayer has paid us to do), trash never sits on the ground waiting for the next day's detail, and everyone is equally invested. How does this philosophy work?

Under the 'if you see it, you own it' philosophy anyone coming upon trash simply stops, bends down, picks up the trash and deposits the trash in the nearest trash can. No magic required ... it really is very simple. If you see it, you own it!

The key to this philosophy is the expectation that everyone is invested—everyone stops to pick up trash when they see it AND more importantly, everyone is willing to call out anyone who walks past trash.

So, when I'm walking on my base or through my yard (or anywhere else for that matter) if I see trash on the ground I pick it up (amazingly simple). Of course, if I see someone walk past trash it is still my duty to stop, pick up the trash, catch up to the individual who walked past the trash and remind them (sometimes with a gentle kick in the ass) of our community's basic philosophy – If you see it, you own it!

You Own Your Own Morale

A while back, I was speaking with a few Senior Airmen[7], who having been selected for promotion were now preparing to 'sew on' Staff Sergeant. I heard some very good things from these soon-to-be NCOs. They told me they want leadership from their leaders. They want honest feedback on their efforts, not flowery BS that does nothing to help them grow. They want leaders who won't shy away from telling it like it is and how it needs to be. They want leaders who'll reward them when they do well, but they especially want leaders who are willing to kick them in the ass when they need that too. They want standards set and then applied to all--- they're tired of seeing people cherry pick jobs/tasks, deployments, or assignments. They're REALLY tired of seeing weak leaders stand by and do nothing about it or worse yet, condone it. Bottom line: They want leaders who'll show them how to be NCOs.

When our conversation broke up, one Airman stayed behind to ask me what I did to keep myself motivated every day. Apparently he saw me as someone who consistently came across as happy to be here and he wondered how I did it.

I told him, **"YOU** own **YOUR OWN** morale!" It is that simple. Don't wait for the one day pass (day away from

---

[7] Senior Airman (SrA) – The senior-most grade in the Airman tier. A skilled technician and trainer, developing supervisory and leadership skills in preparation to serve as a future NCO

duty), the choice assignment, or for some other 'bone' to be thrown your way before you're prepared to be happy about yourself, your career, or your lot in life.

No one can bring you down if you refuse to be brought down. You may be given a Christmas/New Years deployment or an assignment to the last place on Earth you'd volunteer to go, **BUT** no one but **YOU** decides how you're going to feel about it. No one can force you to be negative about anything. So, don't do it. Refuse to be negative! Don't allow the actions (or inaction) of others to bring you down or to cause you to lose your desire to be here. Gravitate toward those with positive attitudes ... try to help those with negative attitudes. Carry them as far as you can. If they catch on before you get tired, great. If not, jettison them to wallow in their own negativism and move on.

Each day I wake up knowing I'm part of something bigger than myself. I'm part of an organization of great Americans on the most noble of missions; to advance the cause of freedom, to eliminate safe havens for terrorists and their supporters, and to save American and coalition lives while doing it. How can I not be motivated? I don't have the time or the desire to be sucked in by negative people or attitudes. I'm the only one who gets to adjust my morale switch—first thing every morning I set mine on HIGH. Where do you set yours?

PGA Pro and PB&J

What's it going to take for our unit to attain full operational capability (FOC)[8]? Simply put, we'll need to practice like a Professional Golf Association (PGA) pro and behave like a peanut butter and jelly (PB&J) sandwich. I believe the more we emulate the world's greatest golfers and America's greatest sandwich the more likely we'll reach FOC.

You might ask, "Hey Chief, what are you talking about? We're Airmen not PGA pros." You're right. But, I believe there are at least two significant similarities. First, we're both driven to succeed; differing only in measure of merit. Theirs is a score relative to par, ours is mission assurance in, through, and from Cyberspace. Second, we both need to develop our 'A' game; we both do it by practicing what we're already good at in order to upgrade from 'good' to 'great'! PGA pros do this at the driving range and on the putting green. We do it through exercises and inspector general assessments. Think about it! Our mindset must be the same with the same purpose in mind, to build muscle memory and winning habits on our way to FOC.

We must respond appropriately to CAMs (Coordination Alert Messages) and ODMs (Operational Directive Messages); properly process CCOs (Cyberspace

---

[8] This story was written in August 2010 in preparation for 24th Air Force's Full Operational Capability assessment by the Air Force Space Command Inspector General. Our unit satisfied this final criterion on 11 September 2010

Control Orders) and MTOs (Maintenance Tasking Orders); develop CTOs (Cyberspace Tasking Orders) and CCOs to direct actions intent on assuring the mission in a degraded environment; respond to crises with COAs (courses of action), providing cyber options to enable a selected COA; and effectively coordinate day-to-day and crisis action activities with United States Cyber Command (USCYBERCOM) via our Air Component Coordination Element (ACCE). If that doesn't sound easy, you're right, it's not. If it were, anybody could do it—and not just anybody can—that's what makes you special.

By the way, our adversaries aren't taking a knee or calling a timeout to give us a break just because we're not 100% manned or because we're already up to our necks in meeting Combatant Commander requirements; nor do our adversaries care that we experience never-ending rotations of skilled and unskilled personnel due to PCS, Expiration of Term of Service (ETS), or retirements. To dissuade our adversaries and to defeat our enemies, we must put on our 'game face', bring our 'A' game to our FOC exercise and assessment, and prove we're ready to deliver mission assurance in, through, and from Cyberspace.

Practicing like a PGA pro is not enough. We must also behave like PB&J. Why PB&J? Well, I can't think of a better example of collaboration. Each ingredient is good in its own right, yet also vastly improved upon when teamed with the other. Yet neither ingredient sacrifices its own identity in the partnership. The ultimate teammate! This is how we as Airmen must also behave. We must sharpen our skills individually and then collaborate with our total force and joint partners to achieve FOC. I'll see you at the driving range and putting green (FOC Exercise later this week). I'll be the guy with the PB&J sandwich in his hand.

Never Failed?
Trying Hard Enough?

Rickey Henderson[9] spent 25 years in professional baseball stealing a major league record 1406 bases. If you know a little about base stealing, you know it involves risk … calculated risk. Rickey's managers accepted the risk of failure in order to improve their team's chances of scoring runs, ultimately improving their team's chances of winning more and losing less.

Did you know Rickey Henderson was also caught stealing 335 times, yet another major league record? I often wonder what would have happened had any one of Rickey Henderson's managers failed to support him, chastised him, or instructed him to no longer take risks after any one of his 335 failures. Had his managers established a culture of 'failure is not an option', do you think he would have stolen 1406 bases? More importantly, do you think his teams would have lost more and won less?

I believe accepting calculated risk is the only way we'll improve who we are, what we do, and how we do it (the Wright Brothers would still be on the ground if risks were never taken)—and when risks are taken, mistakes will happen (they trashed a lot of materiel before they ever got off the ground). Keep in mind, risk does not disregard safety and a

---

[9] Rickey Henderson – elected to the Major League Baseball Hall of Fame in 2009; regarded as the sport's greatest leadoff hitter and baserunner

mistake is an action undertaken with the best of intentions from which we learn and do not repeat—it's quite different than an unethical or illegal act like ignoring technical orders because you think you 'know better'.

So, why are so many of us averse to risk-taking? In my experience, we're unsure our leaders will support us if/when we fail. Why? Because we've seen previous risk-takers get their proverbial head handed to them when their risk-taking proved unsuccessful. What's the bottom line? I believe leaders must do more to cultivate a culture more tolerant of failure (failure as an act of commission not omission). By creating a risk-averse environment, leaders doom Airmen and our organizations to operate devoid of the creative, innovative solutions we'll need to advance our next generation Air Force and the Airmen it will require to fly, fight, and win in air, space, and cyberspace.

President Theodore Roosevelt[10] summed up risk-taking perfectly. "… credit belongs to the man who is actually in the arena, whose face is marred by dust and sweat and blood, who strives valiantly, who errs and comes up short again and again, because there is no effort without error or shortcoming, but who knows the great enthusiasms, the great devotions, who spends himself for a worthy cause; who, at the best, knows, in the end, the triumph of high achievement, and

---

[10] President Roosevelt's "Man in the Arena" is an excerpt from his speech "Citizenship in a Republic" delivered at the Sorbonne in Paris, France 23 April 1910

who, at the worst, if he fails, at least he fails while daring greatly, so that his place shall never be with those cold and timid souls who knew neither victory nor defeat."

Today, Air Force leaders are taking calculated risks focused on five priorities: strengthening the nuclear enterprise, partnering with Joint and Coalition forces to win today's fight, modernizing air and space inventories, recapturing acquisition excellence, and developing and caring for Airmen and their families. Mistakes will be made. Success is not assured. Is our future worth the risk? You bet!

Airmen – take calculated risks to improve your unit's ability to accomplish the mission; speak up if you see something that can be done better. Leaders – please support our Airmen's calculated, mission-focused risk-taking efforts; embrace Air Force Smart Operations (AFSO) 21[11] and encourage our Airmen to critique our business practices, never settling for the status quo. Our Air Force is the best on and above our planet, but will only continue to be so if we're willing to take the risks necessary to improve who we are, what we do, and how we do it!

---

[11] Air Force Smart Operations for the 21st Century, or AFSO21, is a term coined by Air Force senior leaders to represent a program to institutionalize continuous process improvement across the Air Force

Seize Your Opportunity

Within days of my arrival at my first duty station in England in 1985, I was hearing stories about our Senior Enlisted Advisor (Command Chief Master Sergeant). The facts and figures differed from story to story, but the overarching theme of each was pretty consistent, the Chief was a legendary figure with superhero-like powers—omnipresent in our unit and on our base.

One afternoon I was sitting in the chow hall eating lunch, when suddenly the Chief sat down at my table. I was stunned—not at all sure what to say. In fact, I wasn't sure if I should say anything at all. He immediately started asking me a lot of questions about who I was, where I was from, which flight I was assigned to, and which section I worked in. Two things struck me right away. One, he sure did ask a lot of questions. And two, he was smooth. He asked questions in a way that put me at ease. He wasn't interrogating me. He was simply interested in learning a little bit about me. And then he asked his last question, a real doozy.

"Airman Slater, what will you do with your opportunity to impact our base?" I thought of only two responses, "huh" and "duh". I wasn't a Commander, a Chief, or a First Sergeant. Nor did I occupy a position of influence. I was just an Airman. "Chief, I'm not sure I understand the question. I'm just an Airman. How can I have an impact?"

"Airman Slater, the number of stripes on your sleeves may indicate level of responsibility and authority, but they don't indicate level of opportunity. Every member of our unit has the opportunity to make an impact. So, the question is what will you do with yours? As a Chief, I've seized my opportunity to make an impact by helping our commander build a collaborative work environment and by articulating the 'why' or 'how come' of his policies and decisions to all of our members. So, how will you seize yours?" I was dumbfounded.

He continued, "Our unit has one Commander, one First Sergeant, and one Senior Enlisted Advisor, but we have hundreds of Airmen—the largest peer group on our base. As an Airman, you can make an impact by knowing the standard and being the example; by leaving everything better than you found it; by generating ideas and being willing to share them; by enforcing standards peer-to-peer; and by networking within your peer group to help each other grow. Can you imagine the impact of hundreds of Airmen if they come together as one? You don't need a lot of stripes to be a difference-maker. You simply need to engage as a member of our unit's broadest, most diverse, and most influential peer group." (Airmen Committed to Excellence (ACE)[12] didn't exist back then, but what a great opportunity for today's Airmen).

---

[12] ACE is a base-level professional networking organization open to all Airmen in grades E1-E4 (our most junior tier of enlisted personnel)

They're On My Feet

I was engaged in a hallway conversation one day with a young NCO about our rules, policies, and expectations and how our best people (ideally) operate to standards (a barometer) even more stringent than those the Air Force imposes (or maybe to standards the Air Force doesn't even impose). Our conversation eventually steered toward why it seems some people will only act if their leader or organization levies a very specific, well-detailed expectation or standard. And even then, many people will spend a lot of time dissecting the language used to outline the standard or expectation to see if it applies to them, somehow hoping they can get out of or avoid the expectation. Worse yet, even when learning it does apply, then putting more energy into finding a way to do the absolute minimum to meet the requirement than it would have taken to far exceed the standard or expectation in the first place.

At the height of our conversation, a senior civilian in our organization came walking down the hall. I took the opportunity to stop him to ask him why in the absence of specific guidance, of no detailed instruction levying an expectation on him in any way, his shoes were always clean, in good repair, and buffed to a high-gloss shine.[13] His answer?

---

[13] Air Force Instruction 36-2903 directs uniformed personnel to wear shined shoes. No such requirement is formally levied on our civilian members

111

"They're on my feet". I'm not sure the NCO and I immediately understood the profound nature of our civilian teammate's comment. How intriguing. This man needed no specific guidance, instruction, or expectation outlined in verbal or written form by any individual or organization of authority to gain his buy-in to the value of professional image. His barometer was his own sense of personal pride.

He already knew the right answer was to ensure his shoes were clean, in good repair, and buffed to a high-gloss shine. After all, they were on his feet.

Looking for a way to determine whether you're part of a high performance organization? Check people's shoes. I bet if your people operate under the "they're on my feet" philosophy, not only will their shoes be 'sharp', but everything they do will be a result of personal pride and self-motivation. They won't be wasting time waiting on specific guidance, policy, and expectations. They'll already be out front simply getting it done.

A 40-inch Waist or Waste?

The year is 2044—the 80th year of my birth, a full 7 years beyond the life expectancy of today's average American male. It is late spring, as I settle into an uncomfortable folding chair in the auditorium of our small town's university. My wife Linda and I have joined our son and daughter-in-law to see our oldest grandson receive his undergraduate degree. We've arrived early; the ceremony isn't scheduled to begin for at least another 45 minutes. Linda says anticipation and excitement are the reasons we're here early, but I know better. We're here early because we need seats up front—our eyes and ears just aren't what they used to be. While Linda circulates among family members, catching up on news that's occurred since we were last together, I sit back in my chair and reflect on times gone by.

Wow, 2044! It's been more than 30 years since I retired from the Air Force and 40 years since Air Force leadership established our service's first meaningful fitness expectations. Unfortunately, I still remember even at the height of our nation's struggle against terrorism, we spent as much time distracted by our fitness test as we spent discussing how to improve our training, our equipment, and our war-fighting tactics, techniques, and procedures. I was disappointed in the narrow view many of us took. When we could have focused on how improved fitness would positively impact our ability to deploy, to operate in some of the most

113

demanding environments on our planet, to manage stress, and to improve our overall health, many of us instead chose to laser-focus on our 'rights' and what was 'fair' or 'unfair'.

Yes, some wanted to argue how a tall person had a 'right' to a larger abdominal circumference[14]. Somehow some felt a 40 inch abdominal circumference was more 'fair' for a taller Airman than a shorter Airman. Now I'm not a math genius, but I don't remember height being a factor in how to determine circumference of a circle.

And, if the abdominal measurement wasn't the source of drama, too many Airmen (of all grades) believed requiring a 75 on a Physical Training (PT) test was a conspiracy against height-challenged, weight-challenged, speed-challenged, and/or strength-challenged Airmen. And the energy expended by some to complain about the 'minimum standards' instituted for each category on 1 July 2010[15]? Yikes!

I'm sure glad our Airmen spent little time whining and instead focused on the volumes of medical evidence showing the negative impact of increased visceral or intra-abdominal fat. Diabetes, heart disease, stroke, and some cancers may not have been as obvious an enemy as terrorists, yet in 2009 each of them killed more Americans than terrorism.

---

[14] An abdominal measurement is one of four tested fitness components along with a 1 ½ mile run, push-ups, and sit-ups
[15] You can no longer pass the test by relying on outstanding performance in one component to overcome poor performance in another component

I wonder how many extra anniversaries I've been around for, how many extra birthday candles I've blown out and how many extra Christmas gifts I've enjoyed over the years due to Air Force leadership instituting a robust fitness program at the start of the 21st century. As a 6'2" Airman, had I disregarded their efforts and argued for my right to a 40 inch abdominal circumference, would I be here for my grandson's graduation today? Oh, I've got to go, the ceremony is about to begin...................

Starship Troopers

"Chief, what books on leadership should I be reading?" This question was posed to me quite a few years ago by an Airman following an address I made to an ALS[16] class. I'm not sure which titles he was expecting me to suggest, but you should have seen the look on his face when my list started with *Starship Troopers*,[17] the Sci-Fi classic authored in 1958 by Robert Heinlein. Fortunately, he didn't immediately run off thinking I was nuts. Instead, he stuck around to allow me to explain why I recommend this book to every aspiring leader.

When I returned home that evening, I couldn't shake my conversation with this Airman from my head. I searched my house for my heavily dog-eared copy of the book (it had been a while since I last read it cover-to-cover). When I picked it up, out fell a sheet of paper on which I had long ago penned a list of questions the book either answered for me or issues it had shaped my perspective on. I've listed a few of these below.

Is it possible that one person can completely shape your sense of purpose/value in one short conversation? Are conditions ever as impossible as they first appear? Aren't we all capable of overcoming more than we initially give ourselves

---

[16] Airmen attend Airman Leadership School (ALS) in preparation for advancement to NCO grades and assumption of supervisory responsibilities

[17] Starship Troopers – a military science fiction novel written by Robert A. Heinlein; first published in 1959

credit for? Do we do an Airman any favors by withholding a firm and immediate response to unacceptable behavior? Do senior leaders need to be in on every correction? How might I handle a current-day leadership challenge, like someone trying to get me or one of my Airmen to sign 'sight unseen' (pencil whipping) a 'jacked-up' equipment account?

Of course, not only do I encourage you to read the book, but I also wonder if you'll agree or disagree with none, some, most, or all of the answers or perspectives I drew from the book. I suspect you may even build a list of your own answered questions. Was it Robert Heinlein's intention to pen a simple Sci-Fi novel for the casual reader or did he plan to craft a virtual manual on leadership, followership, and civic responsibility by using the Sci-Fi genre as the medium through which he'd pass his leadership lessons? I'm not entirely sure. However, I certainly did appreciate the discovery of profound lessons within a novel far more interesting and digestible than the classic 'tough-to-read', scholarly leadership textbook. I wonder what you might find if you take the time to track down a copy. I'm looking forward to hearing from you once you've completed your journey through the book!

The Whole Person Concept

Many years ago, as a young NCO, I had an opportunity to participate as a member of an Airman of the Quarter board[18]. This was where I was first introduced to a phrase I've heard a million times since: 'The whole person concept'. This phrase attempts to capture all of the qualities of the ideal Airman: a mentally resilient, physically fit, culturally attuned, technically competent, educated, and unit/community servant; the well-rounded Airman.

Over the years, I've found many misunderstand this concept and interpret it as code for 'college and community service are more important than duty performance'. I assure you nothing could be further from the truth. No class or service project will ever 'outrank' duty performance. We are, and must remain, a 'mission first' Air Force.

The best explanation I've seen of the 'whole person concept' was a stick figure drawn by CMSgt Joe Levigne[19] in an article published in 2003. I'm no artist, but using his model, I'll try to draw you the ideal 'whole person'.

Let's start with the head. I think we'd all agree the ideal head would contain not just a brain, but a brain full of knowledge recognized by a CCAF degree in an Airman's

---

[18] Each quarter most units hold a competition to determine the unit's superior performers; this competition often includes a "face-to-face" meeting with a panel of your seniors
[19] Former Command Chief, 2d Bomb Wing, Barksdale AFB, LA

current Air Force Specialty and THEN for extra credit, professional certification, an undergraduate degree, or an advanced academic degree. The ideal enlisted brain would also know The Little Brown Book (AFI 36-2618) is THE enlisted roadmap to being a whole person.

As we move to the torso, I think we'd agree just as the human torso contains vital organs like the heart, liver, and lungs, our whole person torso should contain those things vital to a successful Air Force career; a laser focus on resiliency and fitness (mental and physical), adherence to standards (even those you don't personally agree with), safety (even when no one is looking), and military image (even when you're away from your installation).

Finally, we get to the limbs. Not only do we need four limbs, but our limbs ought to be in proper proportion too; same length and same muscular structure. If one arm is engagement in your unit and installation (active membership in booster club, advisory council, and grade appropriate professional organization (ACE, 5/6, Top 3, Chiefs Group, Company Grade Officer Council (CGOC)), then the other arm must be engagement in your community (scouting, neighborhood associations, church, youth groups, sports leagues, and schools). If one leg is technical competence (Initial Qualification Training (IQT), Mission Qualification Training (MQT), on-the-job training, Career Field Education and Training Plan (CFETP) core tasks, successful upgrade training, and combat skills training), then the other leg must be Airmanship competence (combat readiness, grade-appropriate Professional Military Education (PME) completion, professional reading (CSAF reading list is a great start), and active participation in professional development of yourself and others).

The whole person concept is a simple way to help us see how and why the Air Force values and promotes the well-rounded Airman over the Airman with the empty head, unhealthy torso, disproportionate muscle structure, or uneven limbs. If you drew a stick figure of yourself, would you be a 'whole person'? If your drawing needs professional help, stop rationalizing your stick figure's current condition, and talk to your supervisor today about how to get your stick figure in shape!

Slay Promotion Myths

Last month[20], Air Force leadership announced 7,752 Staff Sergeants had earned promotion to Technical Sergeant, a promotion selection rate of nearly 21 percent. Within moments of this promotion announcement, I guarantee you many disappointed NCOs were trying to figure out where things went wrong for them. In my experience, too many people glaze over the facts and immediately use these two myths to rationalize their non-selection:

MYTH #1: I didn't get promoted because I have a '3' or '4' Enlisted Performance Report (EPR)[21] in my record

FACT: Plenty of people with 3s or 4s get promoted

How do I know? This year's promotion statistics indicate the average person selected for promotion earned 133.11 points from EPRs (that's less than the 'full marks' of 135 points all 5s would have earned). Therefore, some of the people promoted must have had 3s and/or 4s somewhere in their record. Bottom line: Some of our selectees didn't 'max out' their EPR points and they still got promoted. Yes, it's do-able.

---

[20] I first shared this story in June 2009
[21] EPRs are annual reports which earn a numeric grade for performance (1-5) with each grade earning points toward promotion based on a mathematical formula

MYTH #2: My test scores won't matter if my EPRs aren't '5s'

FACT: The Skill Knowledge Test (SKT) and Promotion Fitness Examination (PFE) matter most

How do I know? The total number of points available under the Weighted Airman Promotion System (WAPS) is 460 (for promotion to E-5/E-6/E-7). EPR points 'max out' at 135/460 or 29% of the total score. However, the SKT and PFE 'max out' at 200/460 or 43% of the total score. Therefore, for promotion to E-5/E-6/E-7 your test scores have more impact than your EPRs. Bottom line: If you're not studying, you're wrong!

You don't think you can make up ground on your peers when promotion testing? Think again. Most of your peers are inadvertently giving you every opportunity to pass them by. The average test scores of those selected for Technical Sergeant this year were 57% (SKT) and 71% (PFE). In other words, of 200 possible points, even the people selected only earned 128---if you're willing to out-study your peers, you've got 72 points of opportunity to overcome a record of EPRs less than all '5s'.

What's my point? You CAN get promoted to E-5/E-6/E-7 without a record of all '5s'. In fact, I believe supervisors should spend more time encouraging people to hit the books and less time feeding the myth that a 3 or a 4 (or multiple 3s/4s) will prevent a promotion or ruin a career. In fact, I know of a unit whose promotion rates to TSgt and MSgt in 2009 were triple those in 2008. How did that happen?

Unit leadership recognized they were spending 99% of their time talking about the impact of EPRs on promotions (29%) and only 1% of their time talking about the impact of studying for the PFE/SKT (43%). They chose to stop feeding promotion myths and elected instead to slay them by reversing their order of emphasis ... and voila!

Embrace Development Expectations

I need your help articulating a message. Based on feedback I've received regarding Enlisted Performance Report (EPR) endorsement and award/decoration levels, I get the impression some of us believe CCAF and SNCO Academy by-correspondence are two things SNCOs complete ONLY to secure a senior rater endorsement on an EPR. The thought process being if one is not interested in future promotion, completion of CCAF and/or SNCOA is unimportant, maybe even unnecessary.

NOTHING COULD BE FURTHER FROM THE TRUTH!

If we, as an enlisted force, have a prayer of meeting technological, managerial and leadership challenges in today's and tomorrow's expeditionary force, we must have well-trained, educated and professional senior enlisted leaders. CCAF and SNCOA are two things (and NOT the only two) that will help us to get there. The Air Force expects Airmen to complete a CCAF degree for the career-field proficiency and credibility the degree brings ... NOT because a Wing Commander won't sign an EPR without it. By the way, according to CCAF statistics, the average CCAF graduate is a SSgt with 10 years in service (makes you wonder why we're still having this conversation with a MSgt with more than 15 years or more time-in-service).

The Air Force's single-most useful professional military education tool to prepare our newest SNCOs for the

124

increased leadership and management expectations placed upon them is the SNCO Academy by-correspondence. Thank goodness it's available by correspondence, so our folks aren't cheated out of this opportunity to become stronger while waiting for in-residence slots. Can you imagine if our newest SNCOs had to walk around blind until given the opportunity to attend in residence?

The Air Force wants a TSgt with a line number to MSgt to immediately enroll in and complete SNCOA by correspondence for the increased leadership and management skills course completion brings ... NOT because a Wing Commander won't sign an EPR without it. Our BEST people would not require convincing to enroll in and complete this course would they?

AFI 36-2618 goes to great lengths to help each of us understand the basic responsibilities of each tier of the enlisted force. Each of us is required to meet these expectations (cherry picking is not an option). SNCOs and their supervisors should pay particular attention to pages 13-15[22] of AFI 36-2618. I hope you'll help me to help our folks understand that CCAF and SNCOA completion are basic expectations. By the way, mission expertise or technical know-how (which is critical in its own right) can NOT overcome the leadership shortfalls of a SNCO who has failed to complete basic expectations (of

---

[22] Pages 13-15 of AFI 36-2618 *The Little Brown Book* address SNCO responsibilities

which CCAF and SNCOA are two critical pieces). The Air Force has a name for its most proficient, technically-savvy folks who have not completed CCAF and/or SNCOA ... it's TSgt ... NOT MSgt. I hope you'll work with me to ensure we educate our force on this critical leadership issue.

Reading is Fundamental

As a boy growing up in New York, one of my earliest memories surrounding the significance of reading was seeing the 'book mobile' and television commercials sponsored by an organization called _Reading is Fundamental_ (RIF)[23]. Their very clear message of how reading can be one of the best self-improvement tools is as true today as it was more than four decades ago when RIF first began distributing free books to inner-city kids through a national, grassroots effort of volunteers. While RIF has been focused on the reading habits of elementary school children, I believe their message is just as valid for adults, even Airmen.

Senior Air Force leaders have gone to great lengths to educate us on our service's priorities of Partner with the Joint & Coalition Team to Win Today's Fight; Strengthen the Air Force nuclear enterprise; Develop and care for Airmen and their families; Modernize our Air and Space inventories, organizations, and training; and Acquisition excellence.

With that said, it is not enough to simply know our service's priorities and how each of us fits in. Our success in the 'long war' hinges on our ability to better understand how the world around us (past and present) has shaped, and continues to shape, the beliefs, motives, and intentions of friends and adversaries alike.

---

[23] Reading is Fundamental (RIF) is the oldest and largest children's literacy nonprofit in the United States

Are we as aware of the similarities and differences that exist between people as we should be? Is there something we can learn to improve our ability to conduct our mission? Reading is a great way to learn. I recommend you start with items from the Chief of Staff of the Air Force's reading list[24]: http://www.af.mil/library/csafreading/. After all, reading is fundamental.

---

[24] General Ronald Fogleman created the CSAF Professional Reading Program in 1996 to develop a common frame of reference among Air Force members and to help all Airmen become better, more effective advocates of air and space power. Each CSAF since then has enhanced and continued the Professional Reading Program

Grasp the Baton of Enlisted History

Each year, on 25 June we celebrate the anniversary of the start of the Berlin Airlift (Operation Vittles). Many of you have undoubtedly heard and seen stories commemorating what arguably stands as the 20th century's most impressive air mobility feat. In 1948, a fledgling United States Air Force began a 15 month commitment to sustain the lives of over two million people. During the Soviet Union's land blockade of Berlin, Allied Airmen completed 300,000 sorties delivering nearly 250,000 tons of food and fuel to the people of a city cut off from the world.

Much of the military and popular success of the airlift is attributed to two men, Major General William Tunner, who devised the precise scheduling of flights transiting the only three air corridors into and out of Berlin, and Lieutenant Gail Halvorsen, known to Berliners as the 'Candy Bomber'. There is however, one more name I'd like to point out to you – Corporal Bert Jordan. If you've read *The First Heroes*, watched *30 Seconds over Tokyo*,[25] or read or watched any other books or films depicting the successful 'Doolittle Raid', you may recognize the name Corporal (CPL) Bert Jordan as one of the 28 enlisted members who were 'Doolittle Raiders'.

---

[25] In the book and the film, Ted Lawson gives an eyewitness account of the training, the mission, and the aftermath as experienced by his crew and others that flew on the Doolittle Raid of April 18, 1942

Need to get a B-25 off a rolling carrier deck? Need it to fly more than 600 miles to Tokyo? Then hope by stuffing it full of 5-gallon gas cans you'll have enough fuel to make it to China? Need the crew to bail out over China and avoid capture by the Japanese? No problem, CPL Bert Jordan (Crew #4 engineer/gunner) is there. Oh, you want more?

Six years later, you need to sustain a city of over two million people for 15 months by delivering all of its fuel and food by air? No sweat, Bert Jordan (now a crew chief) is there!

I am humbled to know I have my hands on the 'baton of enlisted history' passed to me from the hands of Airmen like CPL Bert Jordan. Do I feel a sense of honor and purpose? You bet I do. The proud enlisted men and women of our Air Force's previous generations are counting on today's enlisted Airmen to perform their duty just as CPL Jordan did.

Each of us contributes to our legacy, whether you're an Airman or a Chief. Today, as members of the Air Force, we launch sorties in defense of our homeland, we serve as 21st Century sentinels watching over our warriors in combat, we deploy forward to engage the enemy, and we stand ready to answer our nation's call to deliver air supremacy over any point on the globe at a moment's notice. I'm certain if CPL Bert Jordan were alive to visit with our Airmen today, he'd say, "today's Airmen rock!" And he'd be right!

Our Proud Air Force History

On 7 December (the anniversary of the Japanese attack on Pearl Harbor) each year you will undoubtedly hear, read, and see many stories commemorating events surrounding what arguably stands as the 20th Century's most infamous sneak attack. Many of these stories will focus on the heroic actions of soldiers, sailors and Airmen on the day of the attack. I'd like to focus on a story I believe all Airmen should know and be proud of—a story of our Air Force's heroic response.

Let me start by saying if you believe Joint and Coalition Operations is a 21st Century creation or is something our Air Force has only recently begun doing out of necessity due to political pressure, budgetary concerns, or equipment and personnel shortages you'd be wrong.

Immediately following the "day which will live in infamy", our President and senior military officers began crafting a plan to strike back at Japan. This strike, famously remembered as 'The Doolittle Raid', required cooperation between U.S. Army Air Forces, the U.S. Navy, and China's political and military leaders--this was joint and coalition operations seven decades ago—and it worked!

What did this audacious plan require? To fly sixteen Army Air Forces B-25 bombers off the deck of an aircraft carrier (never been done before), to drop ordnance on predetermined Japanese targets (never been done before), to continue on to the Chinese mainland where they'd land at

Chinese airfields (never been done before), to complete a flight plan covering nearly 2,500 miles (never been done before). Air-to-air refueling would have been helpful, but it didn't exist at that time. No, they stuffed those bombers full of 5-gallon gas cans to top off the tanks in flight (I'm serious).

There's much more to the story of this 20th Century Joint and Coalition Operation. Separation from family, crews bailing out over China, ditching aircraft in the sea, surviving internment in Japan and Russia, and more. I highly recommend you read *The First Heroes* authored by Craig Nelson, to learn more about the heroic actions of the 52 officers and 28 enlisted Airmen known as the 'Doolittle Raiders'.

I am humbled to learn stories such as this one and proud of my Air Force's history. Do I feel a sense of honor and purpose? You bet. And, I believe you should too. Each one of you contributes to our legacy, whether you're an Airman (E-1) or a General (O-10). The proud men and women of our Air Force's previous generations are counting on us to perform our duty just as they did. No more. No less.

Our Air Force stands ready to participate in joint and coalition operations not because it's a 21st Century buzz word describing something new or different, but because we've been there, done that, and know it works! To fly, fight, and win in Air, Space, and Cyberspace—our proud Air Force history!

Why are Windshields Larger than Rear View Mirrors?

When I was a young NCO making my fair share of mistakes, my supervisor would often say, "there's a reason why your windshield is larger than your rear view mirror." As you might expect, my response the first few times I heard him say this was to walk away, shake my head, and wonder what the heck he was talking about.

Then one afternoon after I had completely jacked up that day's mission (yes, I've made mistakes and still got promoted to Chief—it is possible), he said it again. "There's a reason why your windshield is larger than your rear view mirror." Instead of walking away this time, I stopped him and asked "what on Earth are you talking about?"

He said, "Kevin, every one of us makes mistakes. In fact, some of our strongest performers have made more than a few mistakes. What separates them from everyone else is they learned from their mistakes, they incorporated what they learned into how they approached their next opportunity, and they never let the job behind them distract them from the job in front of them." I'm not sure if he saw smoke coming out of my ears or if my eyes were glazed over, but he paused for a moment when I must have looked like I needed a chance to digest what he just said.

I thought to myself, "ok, our strongest performers have made mistakes ... they've learned from their mistakes ...

they've incorporated lessons learned ... they didn't let past performance distract them from the task at hand. Ok, I think I get it."

He then went on to say, "Your rear view mirror is important. If used properly, it affords you opportunities to not only see the past, but to learn from it too. However, it's small for a reason. It deserves some attention, but it shouldn't be your focus. Why is your windshield larger than your rear view mirror? You need a wide field of view to clearly see all of today's challenges and opportunities, and our leaders' vision for tomorrow. If you're to be a great NCO you'll need to keep your eyes in front on what's most important; glancing into your rear view mirror only often enough to ensure you shape your future with help from your past."

To this day, every time I look into my rear view mirror I see a lot more than the objects behind me. I see the opportunities I've had. I see my triumphs and I see my failures. Once my eyes return to my windshield, I'm reminded of the real value of those objects in my rear view mirror – each has prepared me in a way to make better decisions, to take more precise actions, and to view with greater clarity and wisdom today's opportunities and tomorrow's challenges.

CONCLUSION

Throughout my career, I've often been described as 'old school', 'hard core', and 'ate up'. My attitude has been shaped by every subordinate, peer, supervisor, First Sergeant, Chief, and Commander with whom I've crossed paths. Each has contributed to a set of beliefs that have given me the passion needed to look forward to every duty day. Sometimes that passion comes across as 'ate up', 'hard core', or 'old school'. In fact, one of my previous First Sergeants (SMSgt Ken Simonton) used to say, "Old school is good school." And, as far as I'm concerned he's absolutely right. I believe regular attendance at Old School would benefit all of us. Here are a few other things I believe:

I believe the strength of our service comes from our core values. These clear behavioral expectations of every Airmen (enlisted, officer, and civilian) set the tone for everything we are as citizens and as Airmen. You may choose to see them as an entry or membership fee. If so, what a small price to pay for the privilege of serving in our nation's Air Force.

I believe we must not tolerate any form of discrimination, prejudice, harassment, assault, abuse, or criminal behavior. Each of us should demand to be treated with dignity and respect. Any Airman offended by someone's behavior should immediately confront that behavior by addressing the offender, addressing the chain of command, or by using other available avenues (First Sergeant, Military Equal Opportunity, Chaplain, Inspector General, and the Command Chief).

I believe we should all be proud to be Airmen; disciplined, full of initiative, and team players. Pride should start with the image you present in uniform. Don't spend time looking for the example. It's often easier and certainly better to BE the example!

I believe our Airmen want and deserve direct and honest feedback (formal and informal). It is the best way for our Airmen to learn what our Air Force demands of them and for our Airmen to communicate to us what they expect in return from our Air Force.

I believe the most effective way to organize, train, and equip our Airmen to accomplish our mission is to practice effective leadership. The less we 'baby', 'coddle', or 'hand-hold' and the more we inspire, motivate, discipline, and reward the better off our service will be.

I believe we must effectively train every Airman and arm each with the tools of their trade. We must then 'set the bar' as high as possible. If we've trained them well, armed each with the tools they need, and set a climate of high expectations, our Airmen will excel.

I believe once we have communicated standards and expectations we must then reward superior performance and admonish failure with equal swiftness. When our Airmen do well, we must recognize them by shaking their hand for a job well done or by submitting them for an award for performance clearly above and beyond our expectations. When they don't do well or don't meet standards, we must take corrective action. If we need to conduct 'remedial training' or take disciplinary action—I suggest we do it, reset the bar high, and get them back on track. We're not a one mistake Air Force (by the way, a crime and a mistake are not the same thing).

I believe we must encourage our Airmen to improve themselves through technical/professional training, professional military education, and off-duty education. Then, we need to remind them it's not what they know, but what they DO with what they know. We must lead our Airmen to get involved across their unit, base, and community (in that order). We must develop our Airmen into tomorrow's leaders.

I believe a well-trained, educated, and informed leader will make decisions at their level. If a decision is yours to make, make it. If you're unsure of what to do, seek advice. But never abdicate your responsibility to make the decision. If it's not your decision to make, pass it (along with a recommendation) up the chain for action.

I believe with authority comes accountability. We are accountable to our Airmen and to a chain of command. We must hold ourselves and our Airmen accountable for our actions. We must never apologize for setting high standards and then enforcing them—never apologize for holding our Airmen accountable.

I believe we need to be willing to take chances. I don't think we should throw caution to the wind, but I do believe we must take chances! Chances are we'll improve our mission or the way we care for our Airmen.

I believe leaders accomplish nothing without followers. The most effective followers are not sheep. They ask questions and provide constructive criticism when our leader's directions are not clear or our leader's plans are flawed. Effective followers improve our leaders by compelling them to strengthen their problem solving and/or communications skills. But, agree or disagree, once our leaders digest the follower's feedback and make their decision or announce their plan, effective followers take ownership of the decision or plan. This is called loyalty and it must live inside every follower. We must all possess it, encourage it in others, reward those in whom it is present, and admonish those in whom it is absent.

I believe clear communication is absolutely fundamental. Without it, failure is assured. An informed Airman will know what we are doing, why we are doing it, and how they fit in. There is no value in keeping our Airmen in the dark. We must use face-to-face encounters, roll calls[26], and phone calls to communicate across our organization.

I believe curiosity is absolutely necessary. We must always ask questions and expect our Airmen to do the same! What is my unit's mission? Who do we support? How can we do better? Why does an Air Force Instruction (AFI) say what it says? What rationale is behind the AFI? Is there a better way? We should never sit back and wait to be informed. We must always seek out answers.

I believe we are members of the same team! We need to look beyond our desks, our squadrons, and our wings. We should not operate 'every man for himself'. We must be the best in the world at what we do if we're to accomplish our mission. In fact, the best way to strengthen our capabilities is to team with our sister units, organizations, and services.

I believe every Airman is an 'expeditionary Airman'. Each of us is responsible for our readiness and the readiness of our Airmen. It is our responsibility to keep personnel readiness folders up-to-date, to complete our mobility training requirements in a timely manner, and to ensure our family care plans are set. There shouldn't be anyone among us who is unaware of what is required. Ultimately, each of us is an Air

---

[26] Roll Call - an opportunity for members to present themselves and their equipment for inspection; roll may be called and then daily tasks, important notifications from the previous shift, and other useful information may be shared

Force warrior and must be ready to endure hardships, wherever on the globe our fight may be.

I believe change is good. Now I'm not talking about unjustified change 'for the sake of change'. I'm talking about well-reasoned, purposeful change. I believe we ought to embrace it! Believe it or not, our strongest Airmen thrive on change. From the moment each raised their right hand, our Airmen have been committed to change: changing lifestyle, changing expectations, changing living environments and locales, etc.

I believe we must all practice the principles of Operational Risk Management (ORM), adopt a safety mindset in all we do, and instill that mindset in our Airmen. If we see a dangerous situation, we must be prepared to take action. If we spot someone about to make an unsafe decision, we're obligated to step in. Our Airmen are way too valuable and important to our nation, our Air Force, our units, and especially to our families to not take safety seriously.

I believe we must lead a balanced life … one where our spiritual, physical, social, and emotional needs are met. Each of us should strive to achieve balance and growth in our professional and personal lives and then make it a priority to assist others to achieve the same.

Our shared commitment to our core values and to each other will go a long way toward ensuring our continued standing as the world's finest Air Force. We share an

140

uncommon purpose: a willingness to lay down our lives in defense of the American way of life. We're not simply showing up to work. We're showing up to an opportunity to affect the world we live in. I can think of no better reason for each of us to look forward to every duty day. What do you believe.......?

ACKNOWLEDGMENTS

So many Airmen have influenced my journey from Airman to Chief Master Sergeant and directly contributed to every event described in *Old School is Good School*. Thank you seems woefully insufficient. I trust each of you know the tremendous impact you've had on me as a professional Airman and on me, Linda, and the boys in our personal lives. I'm forever indebted to Nicole Harley, Bridgett Kramer, Karen Butler, Jon Ellsworth, Jim Fowler, Lucrica Gilliam (Cato), Rachel Staub, Rob and Jennifer Casagrande, Sheila Johnson-Glover, Tracy Anderson, Lauren Barboza, Corina Benitez, Kevin Chronister, Brent Grissom, Pat Johnston, Nik Waller, Kay Williamson, Maurice "Molosophy" Arnold, Marco Aldaz, Don Alexander, Bob Benitez, Marc Benkendorf, Brendan Criswell, Scott Dearduff, Al Dowling, Shelina Frey, Don Hatcher, Mike Hedum, Brian Hornback, Kevin Jurgella, Deb Liles, Jim MacKinley, Dave Nordel, Mike Purvis, Vern Putnam, Rick Ricker, Kurt Schueler, Ken Simonton, Todd Small, AC Smith, Bill Spruill, Hope McMahon, Larry Oakes, Keith Andrews, Laura and Tom Disilverio, Judy Chizek, Anthony Dominice, Rick Stotts, Larry Thompson, Bruce VanSkiver, Wally Wachdorf, David Watt, and Generals Mark Barrett, Jim Keffer, Jim Marrs, Matt Molloy, Jake Polumbo, Charles Shugg, Suzanne Vautrinot, Dick Webber, and Larry Wells.

I owe special thanks to those without whom this book would never have been published: Marco Aldaz – if not for your 'A-Grams' I may never have written a single Notice to Airmen (NOTAM). Marc Benkendorf – I learned something from every conversation we had. I always left your office a better Airman and a better person. Al Dowling – There is no better mentor than Command Chief Dowling. Your wise counsel has proven valuable throughout my time serving America's Airmen. Don Hatcher – Your impact may be broader and deeper than you think (Dave Nordel and I have shared many conversations about how lucky we've been to be led by you). Kurt Schueler – You were the perfect sounding board for me during the many hours we spent in deep, critical thought (I still want your recipe for Guinness pancake syrup). Bob Benitez – my absolute brother in arms. I can think of no better time than the many hours we've spent together on and off the course. My golf game is no better, but I know I'm a better man having known you. Brent Grissom and Vern Putnam – I miss the AFIWC days. In fact, what I miss most is the near-perfect, collaborative environment we enjoyed while building the next generation of Airmen. Whatever help this book may provide to current and future leaders is a direct result of my good fortune in having met and worked with every one of you. Linda – no man has a better partner, no child has a better Mother. Our Air Force owes you a tremendous debt of gratitude. You have improved the lives of so many Airmen and their families.

ABOUT THE AUTHOR

Chief Master Sergeant Kevin Slater has served as an American Airman for almost three decades. He has served as a Command Chief Master Sergeant three times at the Wing and once at a Numbered Air Force. Chief Slater has served overseas during the Cold War and in the United States Central Command Area of Responsibility engaged in Operations IRAQI FREEDOM and ENDURING FREEDOM following the events of 9/11.

22943711R00080

Made in the USA
Charleston, SC
07 October 2013